Countering Russian Social Media Influence

Elizabeth Bodine-Baron, Todd C. Helmus, Andrew Radin,
Elina Treyger

For more information on this publication, visit www.rand.org/t/RR2740

Library of Congress Cataloging-in-Publication Data is available for this publication.
ISBN: 978-1-9774-0182-3

Published by the RAND Corporation, Santa Monica, Calif.
© Copyright 2018 RAND Corporation
RAND® is a registered trademark.

Support RAND
Make a tax-deductible charitable contribution at
www.rand.org/giving/contribute

www.rand.org

Preface

This report documents research and analysis conducted as part of a project entitled *Combatting Russian Social Media Information Operations in the United States*. The purpose of this project was to formulate specific and actionable approaches and policies for countering Russian disinformation on social media inside the United States.

RAND Ventures

RAND is a research organization that develops solutions to public policy challenges to help make communities throughout the world safer and more secure, healthier and more prosperous. RAND is nonprofit, nonpartisan, and committed to the public interest.

RAND Ventures is a vehicle for investing in policy solutions. Philanthropic contributions support our ability to take the long view, tackle tough and often controversial topics, and share our findings in innovative and compelling ways. RAND's research findings and recommendations are based on data and evidence, and therefore do not necessarily reflect the policy preferences or interests of its clients, donors, or supporters.

Funding for this venture was made possible by the independent research and development provisions of RAND's contracts for the operation of its U.S. Department of Defense federally funded research and development centers.

Contents

Figures and Table

Figures

Table

Summary

In January 2017, the U.S. intelligence community released a public report detailing a Russian influence campaign, ordered by Russian President Vladimir Putin, "aimed at the U.S. presidential election."[1] Part of a larger multifaceted approach, this campaign included social media–based disinformation spread by both automated bots and paid trolls. Russia's strategy was to push several conflicting narratives simultaneously, deepening existing divisions within American society and degrading trust in Western institutions and the democratic process.[2] While it is unknown what impact the campaign might have had on the 2016 presidential election, or on individual opinions, it is clear that Russia's efforts reached many Americans through a variety of social media platforms, including Twitter and Facebook.[3]

This report analyzes different approaches and policy options to respond to the specific threat of Russian influence on social media in the United States. To do this, we surveyed relevant literature to under-

---

[1] Office of the Director of National Intelligence, *Assessing Russian Activities and Intentions in Recent US Elections*, Washington, D.C., ICA 2017-01D, January 6, 2017, p. ii.

[2] Unless otherwise noted, we use "Russia" as shorthand for the Russian Federation, its institutions, and its proxies.

[3] We note that Russia has achieved at least one objective through these efforts: increased perception that Russia is skilled at influence operations. As our colleague Dr. Rand Weitzman noted, the numbers of (1) hearings held on this subject, (2) lines of print media, (3) online lines of text and discussions on social media, (4) minutes of airtime on news and other talk shows, and (5) workshops and meetings devoted to this subject (including this project) clearly indicate that the perception of Russia as a "master of the art of influence operations," and the power of such efforts, has increased. See Alexis C. Madrigal, "15 Things We Learned from the Tech Giants at the Senate Hearings," *Atlantic*, November 2, 2017.

stand what solutions have already been proposed through academic articles, think tank reports, the news media, legal journals, or other sources. From this survey, we developed a broad framework—a *disinformation chain*—to analyze the threat posed by Russian disinformation operations on social media and an initial set of solutions. We then convened over 50 subject-matter experts (SMEs) from both the public and private sectors at a workshop hosted at the RAND Corporation office in Washington, D.C., on May 29, 2018, to discuss approaches to address each link of the Russian disinformation chain.

The Russian Disinformation Chain

To lay out the various options and match them to the threat of Russian disinformation operations on social media, we proposed a framework illustrating the chain of Russia influence operations, from Russian leadership, to Russian organs and proxies, through amplification channels, and finally to consumers—a stylized model of a complex dynamic process. Figure S.1 illustrates the four links in the chain, and who—and what—is in those links.

Current Efforts and Proposed Solutions

Current efforts to combat Russian disinformation operations on social media are fragmented and incomplete. Most focus on increasing transparency of political ads, which, while a significant part of the problem, addresses only one facet of the issue. Efforts to increase cooperation and information-sharing are nascent and lack the necessary resources and authorities to make much of a difference. Solutions are independently proposed (and sometimes implemented) by different stakeholders, but rarely are such stakeholders aware of what others are doing, to say nothing of paths of cooperation. Therefore, these solutions cannot be truly effective. Additionally, efforts and potential solutions are complicated by the interpretations of applicable laws and current policies relating to privacy, and the ability of the U.S. government to message

Figure S.1
Russian Disinformation Chain

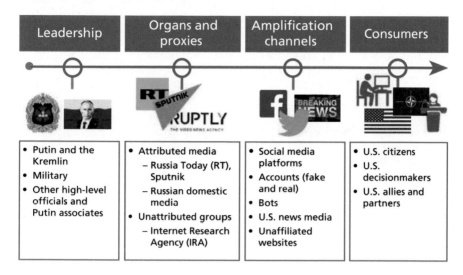

Leadership	Organs and proxies	Amplification channels	Consumers

• Putin and the Kremlin
• Military
• Other high-level officials and Putin associates
	• Attributed media
	  – Russia Today (RT), Sputnik
	  – Russian domestic media
	• Unattributed groups
	  – Internet Research Agency (IRA)
		• Social media platforms
		• Accounts (fake and real)
		• Bots
		• U.S. news media
		• Unaffiliated websites
			• U.S. citizens
			• U.S. decisionmakers
			• U.S. allies and partners

its own citizens. U.S. legal authorities make it difficult for military and intelligence organizations to monitor, collect, or analyze social media information.[4] Moreover, government entities are often explicitly banned from collecting or analyzing social media content produced by private companies. As it currently stands, there does not appear to be a strategy that delineates tasks and responsibilities for an organized response to Russian disinformation operations in the United States— as one official explained during the SME workshop, the U.S. lacks "a real policy mission to counter Russian disinformation."[5]

Proposed Solutions

We focused our discussion of solutions to address the different links in the Russian disinformation chain, from shaping Moscow's lead-

---

[4] For an overview of some of these difficulties, see William Marcellino, Meagan L. Smith, Christopher Paul, and Lauren Skrabala, *Monitoring Social Media: Lessons for Future Department of Defense Social Media Analysis in Support of Information Operations*, Santa Monica, Calif.: RAND Corporation, RR-1742-OSD, 2017.

[5] Unless otherwise noted, quotes within this report are taken from the SME workshop that took place at the RAND Corporation's Washington, D.C., offices on May 29, 2018.

xii   Countering Russian Social Media Influence

ership to limiting Russian proxies, reducing amplification channels, and finally improving consumer knowledge and judgment. Table S.1 summarizes the proposed approaches by links in the disinformation chain. We note that no single approach is likely to be completely effective; rather, a comprehensive and complementary suite of strategies is needed to address all the links in the disinformation chain.

Table S.1
Potential Approaches by Link in the Disinformation Chain

Link in Disinformation Chain	Potential Approaches
Russian leadership	• Make it more difficult for Russia's social media operations to succeed, effectively making it harder or more expensive for Russia to launch a successful influence campaign. • Punish Russia as a whole or sanction various actors within Russia. • Shape Russia's future political development by promoting democracy within Russia. • Set clear norms of behavior and undertake various sanctions when they are crossed. • Come to a shared agreement with Russia to limit its aggressive activities.
Organs and proxies	• Better detect and identify Russian proxies. • Publicize entities identified as Russian proxies. • Deter or curtail activities of known Russian proxies. • Define and monitor norms of behavior relevant to media outlets, social media behaviors, and social media platforms to reduce proxies' credibility.
Amplification channels	• Develop and share tools to detect and combat disinformation. • Coordinate detection of disinformation. • Limit spread of disinformation within social media platforms.
Consumers	• Improve consumer judgment through media literacy campaigns. • Work with social media influencers to help inform key audiences. • Study and publicize the impact of social media disinformation.

Recommendations

Because no single approach to countering Russian influence is likely to produce a conclusive victory over the threat, it is prudent to adopt approaches that target multiple links in the chain. Weighing the advantages and disadvantages of the proposed solutions, we see the emergence of several potential approaches that cut across multiple links:

- Establish clear and enforceable norms for acceptable behavior for states and media entities' behavior on social media platforms.
- Coordinate U.S. executive and legislative branch activities.
- Institute a formal organization for information-sharing that includes key players from the U.S. government and private social media companies.
- Increase the transparency of social media platform policies and algorithms for detecting and removing disinformation and malicious behavior.
- Encourage and fund academia to develop better tools for identifying and attributing disinformation on social media.
- Prioritize defensive activities over punishments to shape Moscow's decisionmaking.
- Continuously assess the cost and impact of proposed solutions, relative to the effectiveness of Russia's activities.

We emphasize that, for these approaches and associated policies to have the best chance of producing the desired effect, the U.S. government, nongovernmental organizations, large and small social media companies, media outlets, and academia will need to enthusiastically participate in and support them. Without cooperation and coordination, efforts will remain piecemeal and inadequate, and the United States will remain vulnerable to influence campaigns by Russia and other adversaries.

Acknowledgments

Many individuals from a variety of organizations contributed to this report. We are particularly grateful to all the workshop participants who enthusiastically gave their time and expertise to discuss Russian disinformation and potential policy options, especially Scott Ruston and Nina Jankowicz for their thought-provoking presentations. We also thank several contributors who were unable to attend the workshop but participated in follow-on discussions and provided additional information in their areas of expertise. We acknowledge and thank our reviewers, Christopher Paul and Rand Waltzman, both RAND colleagues, for their thoughtful comments and edits. Finally, we are grateful to the RAND Corporation, which funded this study through RAND Ventures. Any and all errors are the sole responsibility of the study authors.

Abbreviations

AMWG	Active Measures Working Group
CAATSA	Countering America's Adversaries Through Sanctions Act
DHS	U.S. Department of Homeland Security
DoD	U.S. Department of Defense
DoJ	U.S. Department of Justice
DoS	U.S. Department of State
FARA	Foreign Agent Registration Act
FBI	Federal Bureau of Investigation
GRU	Main Intelligence Unit (Russia)
IRA	Internet Research Agency
NDAA	National Defense Authorization Act
NGO	nongovernmental organization
ODNI	Office of the Director of National Intelligence (U.S.)
RFE/RL	Radio Free Europe/Radio Liberty
RT	(previously) Russia Today
SME	subject-matter expert

CHAPTER ONE

Introduction

Russia actively uses propaganda to promote its interests worldwide.[1] Evidence suggests that Russia has deliberately sowed disinformation through a variety of channels to influence populations abroad and in the United States, including a number of detailed accounts of Russian social media activities and cyberattacks on particular U.S. or European organizations.[2] In January 2017, the U.S. intelligence community released a public report that detailed a Russian influence campaign, ordered by Russian President Vladimir Putin, "aimed at the US presidential election."[3] Part of a larger, multifaceted approach, this campaign included social media–based disinformation spread by automated bots and paid trolls.[4] The St. Petersburg–based Internet Research Agency (IRA), which was later named in an indictment that emerged from Special Counsel Robert Mueller's investigation on February 16, 2018,

---

[1] Unless otherwise noted, we use "Russia" as shorthand for the Russian Federation, its institutions, and its proxies.

[2] We note that Russia has achieved at least one objective through these efforts: increased perception that Russia is skilled at influence operations. As one reviewer noted, the numbers of (1) hearings held on this subject, (2) lines of print media, (3) online lines of text and discussions on social media, (4) minutes of airtime on news and other talk shows, and (5) workshops and meetings devoted to this subject (including this project) clearly indicate that the perception of Russia as a "master of the art of influence operations," and the power of such efforts, has increased. See Alexis C. Madrigal, "15 Things We Learned from the Tech Giants at the Senate Hearings," *Atlantic*, November 2, 2017.

[3] Office of the Director of National Intelligence (ODNI), *Assessing Russian Activities and Intentions in Recent US Elections*, Washington, D.C., ICA 2017-01D, January 6, 2017.

[4] ODNI, 2017, p. ii.

appears to have played a substantial role in the influence campaign, although other Russian organizations might have had active roles as well.[5]

Russia's coordinated social media–based disinformation operations and its continued efforts in this area present a significant challenge to policymakers. Russian information operations' interference in U.S. elections poses an immediate and real threat to U.S. democracy. However, how exactly to respond to Russia's campaign is unclear, for several reasons.

First, Russia's strategy is diffuse. In many cases, as detailed in the RAND Corporation's *Firehose of Falsehood* publication, Russia's strategy is to question all narratives and obfuscate facts, rather than push a particular narrative, with the ultimate goal of degrading trust in Western institutions and the democratic process.[6] In other cases, a Russian campaign might have a specific and clear objective, such as avoiding blame for the shootdown of Malaysia Airlines Flight 17 or the poisoning of its former intelligence agent Sergei Skripal and his daughter. Russia also uses a wide range of tools to achieve its goals—including cyberattacks, public messaging, and state-backed media—but the connection between these tools is not always clear. Formulating a specific response to this range of strategies and behaviors can be difficult.

Furthermore, how effective past or future influence campaigns have been or will be, and to what extent it is worth paying costs or accepting risk to respond to Russian campaigns, is also undetermined. It is clear that Russia's effort reached many Americans. Twitter alone has identified 677,000 users who engaged with Kremlin-linked accounts, and some individual IRA-linked accounts, such as @TEN_GOP, had as many as 100,000 followers.[7]

---

5   Adrian Chen, "The Agency," *New York Times Magazine*, June 2, 2015, p. 57; Indictment, *United States v. Internet Research Agency*, Case 1:18-cr-00032-DLF (D.D.C. Feb. 16, 2018).

6   Christopher Paul and Miriam Matthews, *The Russian "Firehose of Falsehood" Propaganda Model*, Santa Monica, Calif.: RAND Corporation, PE-198-OSD, 2016.

7   Bradley Hanlon, "It's Not Just Facebook: Countering Russia's Social Media Offensive," German Marshall Fund of the United States, Alliance for Securing Democracy, April 11, 2018.

Unfortunately, there are few obvious or ready responses to effectively combat this threat. One suggested response, of more-intrusive government regulation of social media, might not necessarily be effective, could harm the economic prospects of social media companies, and is out of line with U.S. law and traditions.

The potential threat of Russian influence operations, however, is here to stay. This calls for a sustained public conversation about potential policy solutions. Since the 2016 election, a number of individual analysts and organizations have generated a menu of options to combat various dimensions of Russian influence operations, including the spread of disinformation through social media.[8] This report seeks to advance that conversation by drawing on the insights of a diverse, cross-sectoral pool of experts to synthesize the more promising of the approaches, as well as to understand their drawbacks and limitations.

Objectives and Approach

This report categorizes and analyzes different approaches and policy options to respond to the specific threat of Russian influence via disinformation spread on social media in the United States. We gathered, evaluated, and synthesized different proposals to make recommendations about the best way for different U.S. actors to respond to this threat. We note that our focus was exclusively on social media, which is important, but is only one part of the larger Russian influence campaign. Social media does not exist in a vacuum, and it will be important to ensure that these approaches take into account the real-world context in which it is embedded.

---

[8]   See, for example, Jamie Fly, Laura Rosenberger, and David Salvo, *The ASD Policy Blueprint for Countering Authoritarian Interference in Democracies*, Washington, D.C.: German Marshall Fund of the United States, Alliance for Securing Democracy, June 26, 2018; Daniel Fried and Alina Polyakova, *Democratic Defense Against Disinformation*, Washington, D.C.: Atlantic Council, February 2018; Robert D. Blackwill and Philip H. Gordon, *Council Special Report No. 18: Containing Russia: How to Respond to Moscow's Intervention in U.S. Democracy and Growing Geopolitical Challenge*, New York: Council on Foreign Relations, January 2018; and Clint Watts, "Extremist Content and Russian Disinformation Online: Working with Tech to Find Solutions," Foreign Policy Research Institute, October 31, 2017.

Given the goal of characterizing and assessing the range of possible solutions to counter the threat of Russian disinformation on social media in the United States, we took the approach of first surveying relevant literature to understand what solutions have already been proposed in academic articles, the news media, legal journals, or other sources. From this survey, we developed a broad framework—a *disinformation chain*—to analyze the threat posed by Russian disinformation on social media and an initial set of solutions.

We then convened over 50 subject-matter experts (SMEs) from both the public and private sectors at a workshop hosted at the RAND office in Washington, D.C., on May 29, 2018.[9] The participants represented academia, the U.S. Department of Defense (DoD), the U.S. Department of State (DoS), media organizations, a variety of think tanks, and private social media companies with a broad range of expertise, including public diplomacy, information operations, media strategy, Russia, and technology. Through a series of large- and small-group moderated sessions, we discussed four categories of approaches, each corresponding to a different link in the disinformation chain: shaping Moscow's decisionmaking, limiting Russian proxies, reducing the impact of amplification channels, and improving consumer knowledge and judgment.

With respect to each approach proposed (within a particular category in smaller group sessions), we asked participants to consider the following questions:

1. Can a given approach be implemented in time to have an impact in the short term (before 2018 electoral cycle)?
2. What does the approach look like?
3. What would count as success for the approach?
4. What are the costs, drawbacks, and/or obstacles of the approach?
5. In view of costs, drawbacks, and obstacles, is the approach feasible?

---

[9] Unless otherwise noted, quotes within this report are taken from the subject-matter experts (SME) workshop that took place at the RAND Corporation's Washington, D.C., offices on May 29, 2018.

6. If the approach is implemented, what is the likelihood of success?

In the remainder of this report, we first discuss the framework—a disinformation chain—before turning to the assessment of possible solutions related to the specific links of the disinformation chain. We note that few of the approaches we describe here are novel; rather, we categorize and compare different approaches that have been proposed, weighing their relative merits and drawbacks.

This report is meant to educate and inform U.S. government officials considering policies for combating Russian disinformation; social media companies undertaking efforts to reduce the spread of disinformation on their platforms; nongovernmental organizations (NGOs), think tanks, and academics developing new approaches to address the threat of disinformation; and the American public.

CHAPTER TWO

Disinformation Chain

To analyze the threat posed by Russian disinformation on social media, we developed a framework illustrating the *chain* of Russian influence operations—going from Vladimir Putin to an ordinary "Joe" or "Jane" in America—from Russian leadership, to organs and proxies of the Russian government, to amplification channels, to consumers, as shown in Figure 2.1. We note that this is a very simplified picture of a dynamic, nonlinear process that involves multiple nodes, feedback loops, and other complexities. However, by simplifying the framework to these four basic components, we can illustrate where current and

Figure 2.1
Russian Disinformation Chain

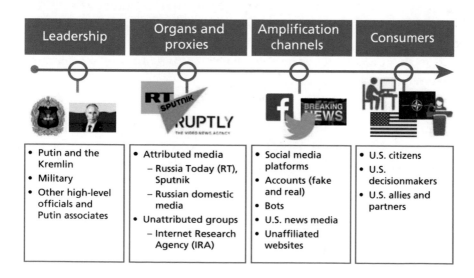

Leadership	Organs and proxies	Amplification channels	Consumers

• Putin and the Kremlin
• Military
• Other high-level officials and Putin associates
	• Attributed media
	  – Russia Today (RT), Sputnik
	  – Russian domestic media
	• Unattributed groups
	  – Internet Research Agency (IRA)
		• Social media platforms
		• Accounts (fake and real)
		• Bots
		• U.S. news media
		• Unaffiliated websites
			• U.S. citizens
			• U.S. decisionmakers
			• U.S. allies and partners

proposed policies to address Russian influence are concentrated, and where gaps might exist.

Russian Leadership

The first step in the chain is the Russian state itself—namely, Russian leadership and the Kremlin. As the Intelligence Community Assessment notes, President Putin "ordered" the influence campaign in the United States.[1] There are questions about how much Russian actors undertaking social media activities are controlled by or coordinated from the top of the Russian government, but it is clear that the influence campaign would not have happened without a high-level decision within Russia's government. Thus, shaping Moscow's decisionmaking offers a key approach to addressing Russian disinformation efforts.[2]

Organs and Proxies of Russia

The diverse organizations that actually implement Russia's influence campaign compose the second link in the disinformation chain. Mark Galeotti observed that "Russia's is a broad-based campaign in which the majority of ventures come from the initiative of individuals within and without the government apparatus, guided by their sense of the Kremlin's desires rather than any detailed master plan."[3] Thus, in addition to shaping Moscow's decisionmaking, changing the behaviors of these proxies is also critical.

---

[1]   See, for example, ODNI, 2017, p. 1.

[2]   We note that policies will need to address the full scope of Russia's leadership, not just Putin. James P. Farwell notes, "Given Putin's unpredictable, distrustful nature, attacking him personally could escalate matters. Characterizing Russia's actions as Kremlin activity makes the point with fewer downsides," from "Countering Russian Meddling in U.S. Political Processes," *Parameters*, Vol. 48, No. 1, Spring 2018.

[3]   Mark Galeotti, *Policy Brief: Controlling Chaos: How Russia Manages Its Political War in Europe*, London: European Council on Foreign Relations, August 2017.

Because these entities are so diverse and operate with varying levels of independence from the Russian government, we organize them into three, potentially four, categories.[4] The first category includes actors who are part of the Russian state, such as the Main Intelligence Unit (GRU) or Sputnik online media.[5] A second category, including entities such as the RT news network, are not formally part of the Russian state but are transparently supported by it. It bears noting that this category includes Americans such as Larry King and Jesse Ventura, both of whom have programs on RT. A third category involves entities that knowingly act on behalf of the Russian government, but whose connections to the state are concealed, such as the IRA (also known as the "St. Petersburg troll factory"), or webpages that do not have clear Russian attribution, but whose funding connects them to the Russian state. A potential fourth category includes entities that, in effect, act to further the purposes of the Russian government but who are not directly connected to the Russian state. We call those in this category *potential* proxies, because it is debatable whether such actors are proxies in a meaningful sense, and whether direct action to counter them would be feasible or desirable. This includes witting and unwitting participants who are motivated to spread messages convenient to Russia's goals for their own reasons—including those simply holding views the Russian government seeks to promote—and therefore provide an additional channel to achieve Russian goals, such as creating or expanding divisions in American society.[6] This category

---

[4] Linda Robinson, Todd C. Helmus, Raphael S. Cohen, Alireza Nader, Andrew Radin, Madeline Magnuson, and Katya Migacheva, *Modern Political Warfare: Current Practices and Possible Responses*, Santa Monica, Calif.: RAND Corporation, RR-1772-A, 2018.

[5] Ellen Nakashima, "Inside a Russian Disinformation Campaign in Ukraine in 2014," *Washington Post*, December 25, 2017. "Sputnik" refers to a Russian state-sponsored media outlet.

[6] According to Andrew Weisburd, Clint Watts, and J. M. Berger,

> Data dump websites, such as Wikileaks and DC Leaks, overtly claim to be exposing corruption and promoting transparency by uploading private information stolen during hacks. But the timing and targets of their efforts help guide pro-Russian themes and shape messages by publishing compromising information on selected adversaries. The people who run these sites do not necessarily know they are participants in Russian agit-

also includes patriotic Russian hackers and networks run by criminal oligarchs. Different approaches to address the influence of different categories could be needed, given the legal status and position of these actors—some of whom are in Russia and others of whom are based in the United States and Western countries.

Amplification Channels

The third link in the chain comprises the various channels (actors and platforms) through which Russian disinformation is intentionally or unintentionally amplified. Social media platforms, such as Facebook and Twitter, play a key amplification role through their policies, algorithms, and advertising—a role that can be manipulated, subverted, or taken advantage of by Russian actors trying to spread disinformation. The accounts that are active on these channels are also particularly important; many play a role in amplifying disinformation, whether they are real or fake, bots, trolls, or regular users.[7] Russian and other foreign contractors who openly offer a variety of social media services for a fee, such as increasing follower counts or posting messages or

---

prop, or at least it is very difficult to prove conclusively that they do. Some sites likely receive direct financial or operational backing, while others may be paid only with juicy information. (Andrew Weisburd, Clint Watts, and J. M. Berger, "Trolling for Trump: How Russia Is Trying to Destroy Our Democracy," *War on the Rocks*, November 6, 2016)

[7]   We differentiate between bots and trolls in the following manner: Bots are accounts that automatically post or retweet, with human direction but without human operation and are often used to make it appear as if a topic is trending when it is not; trolls are accounts that are operated by humans and generally engage in rude conversation or behavior. Fake accounts could be bots or trolls or appear to be innocuous regular users. We note that not all bot accounts have nefarious purposes (for example, news and other aggregator accounts are often useful).

Additionally, users who unknowingly spread propaganda are sometimes referred to as "useful idiots" and sometimes overlap with the potential fourth category of Russian proxies mentioned previously. The key characteristic of this group is that members do not intentionally serve Russia's purpose; rather, they spread information that originates from a Russian proxy for their own purposes, because it aligns with their point of view, for financial gain, for entertainment, or for some other reason.

comments, add an interesting dimension to this link in the chain. Given the variety of openly available Russian social media services, a *plausible* explanation for social media influence campaigns that benefit American interests and that can be traced to Russian accounts is that these campaigns are paid for by U.S. interests and carried out by Russian contractors. An interesting potential example of this kind of social media "service" is when numerous bogus messages appeared on the Federal Communications Commission comment website on the issue of disbanding net neutrality, and the messages turned out to come from Russian sources.[8] As a result, it can be very difficult to link such amplifying channels directly to the Russian state. Finally, U.S. media channels fall into this category, in that they can pick up and spread disinformation.

Consumers

The final link in the chain is the set of targets for a given influence campaign. In our case, the targets are U.S. citizens and decisionmakers. In other cases, the link might include leaders of North Atlantic Treaty Organization (NATO) allies or other governments, or the populations in NATO countries. This link also overlaps with the amplification channels, in that, in many cases, consumers contribute to the spread of disinformation by posting, retweeting, or otherwise promoting such content. Consumers are particularly important to highlight, as any effort to lessen the impact of disinformation at this point in the chain must address human nature—changing algorithms or platforms may reduce the visibility of some disinformation, but, in the end, it is up to the user to believe or not believe a particular piece of content.

In the next chapter, we examine current efforts to address the threat of Russian disinformation and then present proposed solutions and their benefits, drawbacks, effectiveness, and timeliness, based on both the literature review and workshop.

---

[8] Todd Shields, "FCC Got 444,938 Net-Neutrality Comments from Russian Email Addresses," *Bloomberg News*, November 29, 2017.

CHAPTER THREE

Current Efforts and Proposed Solutions

Several government and nongovernmental organizations currently play a role in responding to Russian disinformation. However, despite some coordination through regular meetings and by developing activities within the U.S. National Security Council, there does not appear to be a strategy that delineates tasks and responsibilities for an organized response to Russian disinformation in the United States; as one official at the workshop explained, the United States lacks "a real policy mission to counter Russian disinformation."

In this chapter, we summarize current and ongoing efforts by government organizations and private social media companies based on a literature review and discussion with SMEs, delineating where efforts are concentrated in terms of the disinformation chain discussed in Chapter Two and noting any gaps.[1] We then analyze a variety of proposed policies, examining potential costs, benefits, timeliness, and effectiveness, and suggest where and how such policies could be implemented to reduce the impact of Russian disinformation on social media in the United States.

---

[1] This statement is valid as of the time of writing. Policies in this area are rapidly changing, and newer ones may not be captured in this report.

Current Efforts

Efforts by U.S. Government Organizations

While some U.S. government organizations have specified lead roles for certain tasks related to Russian disinformation on social media, the list of responsibilities below indicates the absence of a clear overall lead agency to coordinate U.S. government activities to respond to Russian disinformation and nefarious actors on social media (or channels).[2]

The U.S. Department of Homeland Security's (DHS's) official role in countering Russian disinformation operations began in January 2018.[3] The department took the lead for risk management relating to elections and other critical infrastructure. Specifically, according to DHS officials, the department is attempting to coordinate information-sharing and partnerships between state and local governments, private sector companies, and federal departments and agencies.[4] The newly formed DHS Countering Foreign Influence Task Force is charged with helping DHS leadership understand the scope and scale of this risk and is working with social media companies, academia, and international partners and across the executive branch on a variety of projects to build national resilience against foreign interference operations.[5] While all these coordination activities could, in theory, help state and local governments act more effectively, they indicate that DHS does not have a direct role in publicly countering Rus-

---

[2]   Importantly, U.S. legal authorities make it difficult for military and intelligence organizations to monitor, collect, or analyze social media information. For an overview of some of these difficulties, see William Marcellino, Meagan L. Smith, Christopher Paul, and Lauren Skrabala, *Monitoring Social Media: Lessons for Future Department of Defense Social Media Analysis in Support of Information Operations*, Santa Monica, Calif.: RAND Corporation, RR-1742-OSD, 2017.

[3]   DHS defines foreign influence operations as malign actions taken by foreign governments or foreign actors designed to sow discord, manipulate public discourse, bias the development of policy, or disrupt markets for the purpose of undermining the interests of the United States and its allies.

[4]   According to an official, "DHS's primary role comes from the domestic partnership capabilities aspect. [The Critical Infrastructure Partnership Advisory Council] construct allows [DHS] to share things that are non-[Freedom of Information Act]-able."

[5]   DHS, "Critical Infrastructure Partnership Advisory Council," September 18, 2018.

sian social media disinformation, nor is it taking the lead in organizing an interagency response.

In July 2018, as part of its Cyber Digital Task Force, the U.S. Department of Justice (DoJ) issued a report proposing an increased role in both investigating threats and informing the public and victims of foreign influence operations.[6] The Cyber Digital Task Force report notes the challenge of cyber threats, as well as covert and overt influence threats, and describes DoJ actions to respond to them, such as briefing potential targets.[7] The Federal Bureau of Investigation (FBI), which is under DoJ, plays an investigative role, including through its Foreign Influence Task Force (FITF), which was created in November 2017. The FBI's role appears focused on cases where there is a clear violation of U.S. law, such as the investigation into the activities of the IRA.

DoS's Global Engagement Center, established in 2016 to counter violent extremist propaganda, is mandated to "lead, synchronize, and coordinate efforts of the Federal Government to recognize, understand, expose, and counter foreign state and non-state propaganda and disinformation efforts aimed at undermining United States national security interests."[8] For a variety of reasons, including funding limitations, these efforts are still in their infancy; also, given DoS's role, these efforts focus on international engagement rather than addressing challenges within the United States.

DoD has a role in combating adversary disinformation in Europe and abroad, but it is limited domestically. However, DoD might be able to provide support to government, private organizations, or both in terms of expertise, intelligence, data, tools, or other resources. We note that the 2018 National Defense Authorization Act (NDAA) directed the Secretary of Defense and Secretary of State to jointly develop a

---

[6] Ellen Nakashima, "Justice Department Plans to Alert Public to Foreign Operations Targeting U.S. Democracy," *Washington Post*, July 19, 2018.

[7] DoJ, *Report of the Attorney General's Cyber Digital Task Force*, Washington, D.C., July 2, 2018.

[8] Public Law 113–328, The National Defense Authorization Act for Fiscal Year 2017, December 23, 2016.

comprehensive strategy to counter the threat of malign influence by Russia, including an approach to counter the use of "misinformation, disinformation, and propaganda in social and traditional media"; but at the time of writing, such a strategy has not yet been published.[9] Nor has any concrete action been taken following the Portman-Murphy Counter-Propaganda Bill that was signed into law as part of the 2017 NDAA and expanded on in the 2018 NDAA.

U.S. Legislation

Current legislative efforts take several approaches. First, as part of a larger policy to respond to hostile Russian actions since 2014, there is an ongoing effort to increase sanctions against Russia, including through the 2017 Countering America's Adversaries Through Sanctions Act (CAATSA) and proposed new legislation.[10] A second approach focuses on improving the transparency of foreign influence and political ads on social media, such as the Honest Ads Act. This approach would require ads on social media to adhere to similar regulations to those that appear on television and radio by disclosing the funding source of the advertisement. Blackwill and Gordon suggest updating campaign finance laws to cover a broader range of online activity, enhance transparency requirements, and prevent political spending by foreign nationals.[11] These proposals share a single approach: taking an existing legislative tool and applying it to the social media space.

Another ongoing effort proposes applying existing cybersecurity policy and legislation to foreign influence operations, in particular, establishing and enhancing information-sharing between relevant organizations.[12] In cybersecurity, the goal is to detect adversary activi-

---

[9]   Public Law 115-91, The National Defense Authorization Act for Fiscal Year 2018, December 12, 2017.

[10]   Karoun Demirjian, "Republicans, Democrats Partner on Russia Sanctions Bill, New Cyber Measures," *Washington Post*, August 2, 2018.

[11]   Blackwill and Gordon, 2018.

[12]   U.S. House of Representatives, *A Borderless Battle: Defending Against Cyber Threats; Hearing Before the Committee on Homeland Security*, Washington, D.C.: U.S. Government Printing Office, March 22, 2017.

ties and coordinate countermeasures; a similar goal applies to information operations. Legislation encouraging public-private collaboration to develop best practices for risk reduction and share information to protect customers would require modification to apply to information operations on social media, but the structure and precedent already exist in U.S. legislation.

Private Social Media Companies

In response to the revelations about Russian "meddling" in the 2016 election, social media companies have pledged to clean their platforms of the accounts that spread disinformation and of the content itself. Facebook has removed 470 inauthentic accounts that were likely operated out of Russia and has recently hired more human curators and partnered with fact-check organizations to keep misinformation out of people's News Feed.[13] In general, Facebook's advertised policy is to follow a "remove, reduce, inform" approach. Content that clearly violates its community standards is removed.[14] Content that is "false or misleading" is reduced, and users are informed about it.[15] All links to news stories are processed through a machine-learning classifier that flags stories as potential misinformation based on a variety of signals, including reactions, comments indicating disbelief, and sources.[16] Potential misinformation is then routed to third-party fact-checkers (to avoid making Facebook the arbiter of truth), and anything rated as a "mixture" or misleading is demoted in News Feed. An article from a verified news source supplied by the fact-checker will also appear beneath the disputed content. This current effort is focused on links to

---

[13] Scott Shane, "The Fake Americans Russia Created to Influence the Election," *New York Times*, September 7, 2017; Adam Santariano, "Government 'Cyber Troops' Manipulate Facebook, Twitter, Study Says," *Bloomberg*, July 17, 2017.

[14] Facebook , "Community Standards," 2018.

[15] Facebook recently expanded the scope of misinformation that could be removed from the platform to include posts that could lead to imminent violence in particular geographic areas. See Hamza Shaban, "Facebook Says It Will Start Removing Posts That May Lead to Violence," *Washington Post*, July 19, 2018.

[16] Dan Zigmond, "Machine Learning, Fact-Checkers and the Fight Against False News," Facebook Newsroom, April 8, 2018.

news stories and continues to be refined, but Facebook plans to expand it to verify images and video.[17] Such efforts are likely to continue, but these efforts cannot address the full scope of Russian information operations and the disinformation chain.

In response to calls for more transparency of political ads, Google, Facebook, and Twitter have all implemented changes in how political ads are displayed. During Ireland's recent abortion referendum, Google banned all political ads that showed a stance on abortion, while Facebook created a transparency tool to see all the ads for a single advertiser and eliminated foreign ads or those originating from an unknown location.[18] In planning for the 2018 U.S. midterm elections, Facebook has stated that it will create a "paid for" link to place at the top of any political ads in the United States.[19] Users clicking the label will be taken to a page where they can see the cost of the ad and the demographic breakdown of the viewing audience.[20] Facebook also plans to keep an archive of political ads for the next seven years or through a full congressional election cycle; these ads will be available to Facebook users.[21] Twitter is pursuing a potentially more aggressive approach, planning to restrict who can run political ads on its service and requiring those running ads for federal elections to identify themselves and certify that they are in the United States, with the goal of preventing foreign nationals from targeting political ads to people in the United States.[22] In addition to these requirements, Twitter plans to

---

[17] Tessa Lyons, "Hard Questions: How Is Facebook's Fact-Checking Program Working?" Facebook Newsroom, June 14, 2018.

[18] Adam Santariano, "Ireland's Abortion Referendum Becomes a Test for Facebook and Google," *New York Times*, May 25, 2018.

[19] This approach does not address the challenge of individual users expressing political opinions (who might in reality be paid to do so), such as the estimated 2 million Chinese "internet commentators" paid by the Chinese government. It remains unclear as to how "political accounts" are to be defined.

[20] Nellie Bowles and Sheera Frenkel, "Facebook and Twitter Plan New Ways to Regulate Political Ads," *New York Times*, May 24, 2018, p. A12.

[21] Bowles and Frenkel, 2018.

[22] Bowles and Frenkel, 2018.

start giving prominent visual cues, such as a badge with a particular logo and disclaimer, to campaign ads. Accounts that are used for political campaigning will be required to have a profile photo and other markers consistent with their campaign.[23] Finally, these accounts and those for any of their advertisers must include in their biography a website with valid contact information.[24]

We note that, without any outside verification, it is difficult to ascertain whether any private company is actually doing what it says it will do, how such changes are implemented, or whether such changes actually work. Most research comes from within the companies themselves, and most outside researchers with access to inside information must sign nondisclosure agreements, limiting the ability for others to validate their work.

Gaps in Current Efforts

Current efforts to combat the dissemination of Russian disinformation on social media are fragmented and incomplete. Most focus on increasing the transparency of political ads; while the lack of transparency is a significant part of the problem, increasing such transparency only addresses one facet of the issue. Efforts to increase cooperation and information-sharing are nascent and lack the necessary resources and authority to make much of a difference.[25] Solutions are independently proposed (and sometimes implemented) by different organizations, but rarely are these organizations aware of what others are doing, much less how to cooperate; therefore, the solutions cannot be truly effective. Additionally, while it may be controversial, something as straightforward as U.S. military or intelligence organizations monitoring and col-

---

[23] However, we note that this approach would only apply to accounts that are openly advertised as affiliated with a particular political campaign and does not address the unattributed campaigning issue.

[24] Bowles and Frenkel, 2018.

[25] Facebook recently convened a meeting with other tech companies, the FBI, and DHS to discuss strategies to combat malicious actors, but specific outcomes of the meeting have not been specified. This information is based on Elizabeth Dwoskin and Ellen Nakashima, "Tech Didn't Spot Russian Interference During the Last Election: Now It's Asking Law Enforcement for Help," *Washington Post*, June 26, 2018.

lecting publicly available social media information is not seen as being possible under Title 10 or Title 50 authorities, and government entities are often explicitly banned from such activities by private companies' terms of service agreements.[26]

The goal of the next section is to lay out the various strategies that could be implemented by various organizations and show how these strategies together address the entire disinformation chain, feeding into each other and comprehensively combating the threat. Some are already in progress, as noted above, but could use additional resources, expertise, or coordination.

Proposed Solutions

In this section, we detail proposed approaches and associated policies to combat each aspect of the disinformation chain, from shaping Moscow's decisionmaking to limiting Russian proxies, reducing amplification channels, and improving consumer knowledge and judgment. No single approach will be completely effective; rather, a comprehensive and complementary suite of approaches and policies are needed to address all the links in the disinformation chain. We note that the majority of these suggestions come from the SME workshop held at RAND on May 29, 2018. When possible, we cite where specific suggestions are also present in the literature.

Shaping Moscow's Decisionmaking

The first set of proposed approaches and policies we examine focus on deterring the front end of the disinformation chain—disinformation planners or the Russian decisionmakers who pursue influence campaigns to extend Russia's influence and reach and reduce the stature of the United States and its allies. We identified promising or plausible

---

[26] Title 10 of the United States Code defines the role of the armed forces, military services, and the United States Department of Defense. Title 50, "War and National Defense," is often used as shorthand to refer to the role of the intelligence community, though it covers far more than just intelligence.

approaches and policies that fit into five categories, which are aimed at the following:

- defense or deterrence by denial
- punishment
- democracy promotion
- norm-setting
- negotiated agreement.

Defend and Deter by Denial

This first approach—referred to as defense or deterrence by denial—attempts to make it more difficult for Russia's social media operations to succeed. This approach would effectively make it harder or more expensive for Russia to launch a successful influence campaign through a variety of means, including increasing the resilience of the U.S. population to influence or making it harder to spread disinformation on social media platforms. In discussions of deterrence, a distinction is sometimes made between *deterrence by denial,* which entails conducting activities prior to an attack to make the adversary believe an attack is less likely to succeed, and *defense,* which involves conducting activities that would take place once an attack occurs. Since Russia's disinformation operations on social media are ongoing, the distinction between these deterrence actions is blurry; actions to make ongoing Russian activities less likely to be effective could also make Russia less likely to pursue future offensives.[27] All (or nearly all) of the policies discussed under the next three phases of the disinformation chain fall under the defense or deterrence by denial approach. For example, the policy of publicizing the activities of Russian proxies makes it harder for these proxies to operate, and hence less likely that Russia might use these proxies in the future. Similarly, improving consumer knowledge, such as by integrating media literacy into high school curricula, as proposed below, may make Russian campaigns less successful, and hence less worthwhile for Russia to pursue in the future. These policies could

---

[27] Glenn Herald Snyder, *Deterrence and Defense,* Princeton, N.J.: Princeton University Press, 1961.

be taken by a range of different actors, including the U.S. government, companies, and NGOs. To fall under the approach of defense or deterrence by denial, such policies would need have the explicit purpose of making Russian social media operations less successful.

The defense or deterrence by denial approach has many advantages and few disadvantages, although, ultimately, its overall effectiveness may be limited. Workshop participants quickly focused on defense or deterrence by denial as their fundamental approach to shape Russia's decisionmaking, partly because improving defense can shape the behavior of nearly all Russian actors in the disinformation chain. Defense activities have the advantage that they may also resolve problems associated with a wider range of U.S. societal problems beyond Russian influence, such as online bullying. Another advantage is that defensive activities carry little risk of an escalating Russian response, because they focus on entities operating within the United States, rather than targeting actors in Russia. Russia could, of course, retaliate against U.S. organizations if the activities of its proxies are curtailed, but there is less risk of Russia striking out because it feels threatened at home.

In terms of disadvantages, defense or deterrence by denial may be costly, and it may not actually change Russia's decisionmaking. No matter how much is done to strengthen defenses, vulnerabilities will likely remain. Even if defensive measures raise the costs for Russia to the point where Russian operations are unlikely to succeed, Russia may nevertheless continue to pursue influence campaigns for domestic political reasons. Different actors within Russia may also have variable perspectives on the cost and benefit of social media–based disinformation, meaning that there is a high barrier for improving defenses to convince Russia not to pursue disinformation campaigns in the future.

Punish Russian Actors

The second strategy is to punish Russia as a whole, or to sanction various actors within Russia. In theory, increasing the costs to the Russian government in general, and Putin in particular, could deter the Russian government from undertaking similar operations in the future. The U.S. government has already initiated several measures to punish

Russia for its role in the 2016 influence campaign, including expelling diplomats, creating new authorities to respond to cyberattacks, maintaining and expanding sanctions, and exploring and in some cases implementing new sanctions on oligarchs and other individuals with close links to the Russian government.[28]

Workshop participants identified a range of alternative policies for punishment. One approach involves "naming and shaming," meaning publicizing bad behavior by Russian actors, whether through an official study (similar to the report of the 9/11 Commission) or a broader diplomatic initiative. Other participants at the workshop urged expanding U.S. in-kind responses to Russian operations, such as cyberattacks or information operations. A third suggested approach was to target Russian economic interests; examples of this might include stopping the Nord Stream 2 natural gas pipeline from Russia to Germany or targeting the Russian financial system. Other analysts have suggested additional ideas for more precisely targeting Putin and his associates, such as releasing information about corrupt activities in Russia.[29]

The advantage of punishment is that it may cause sufficient harm to Putin to convince him not to undertake subsequent efforts. But the actual likelihood of these punishment activities succeeding is difficult to assess. It is impossible to know whether the Russian government would have undertaken additional activities against the United States without the existing punishment or whether greater punishment would have led to greater Russian restraint. Some options for punishment include democracy promotion activities (described in more detail in a later section) or otherwise weakening Putin's hold on power, echoing Soviet-era U.S. tactics of political warfare.[30] One participant recommended a U.S. policy of putting "Russia back to where it belongs,

---

[28] Natasha Turak, "Trump to Agree to New Russia Sanctions but Impact Will Be Minimal, Analysts Predict," *CNBC*, January 28, 2018; Kadhim Shubber, "US Extends Sanctions Deadline for EN+, Rusal and Gaz Group," *Financial Times*, May 31, 2018.

[29] Blackwill and Gordon, 2018.

[30] Robinson et al., 2018, Chapter Two; see also Michael Kimmage's account of Michael McFaul's tenure as ambassador in Moscow as a form of "take that, Putin" policy in "Russian Elegies: Candide Goes to Moscow," *War on the Rocks*, June 13, 2018.

a nation with minimal economic footprint and appropriate with its post–Cold War position. Russia is trying to hit above its weight right now."

Punishment has several disadvantages and risks. First, as one participant noted, sanctions may not be effective because, from his perspective, the impact of sanctions is small, relative to other incentives shaping Russia's decisions. By his account, the Ukraine sanctions, which have been in place for years, were a "blunt, ineffective tool," and the "the prices have to be very high" to convince Russia to change its policy. Another participant similarly observed that sanctions have affected the Russian economy, but not necessarily its policies.

Second, punishment requires attribution, which is currently quite difficult and time-intensive and likely to grow more difficult. Obfuscation techniques continually evolve and improve, and a nation-state with sufficient motivation and expertise, such as Russia, is likely to avidly pursue such technologies.

A third disadvantage of punishment is that it could lead Russia to escalate its activities against the United States. Accounts of Russian foreign policy highlight how Russia is motivated to undertake aggressive actions toward the West because of the perceived threat of Western actions. Any additional Western punishments, especially actions targeted toward weakening Putin's hold on power, are likely to be taken as a direct threat to the regime and lead to escalation. Further, Russia may not distinguish between actions intended as a response to its specific activities on social media and actions intended as a larger Western intent to weaken or cause harm to Russian interests. One workshop participant suggested that the United States could make the linkage clear through informal communications. But many participants observed that the current lack of clear coordination among U.S. government bodies could undermine the impact of deterrence by punishment. Mutual distrust between Russia and the United States could similarly undermine the clarity of message associated with punishment.

A final disadvantage is that U.S. allies may not support punishing Russia, especially European countries who seek to maintain a positive relationship with Russia and who may perceive U.S. actions against Russia as unnecessarily aggressive.

Promote Democracy to Punish Russia and Shape Its Future Behavior

In addition to serving as a means of punishing Russian misbehavior, efforts to spread democratic messages or otherwise promote democracy in Russia could also shape Russia's political development so that the government is less likely to pursue social media disinformation operations, among other influence campaigns, in the future. One participant argued that it was important to "get the truth to the Russian people," as part of an effort to "squeeze Russia from many sides." While there are existing U.S.-led efforts to reach the Russian public, such as Radio Free Europe/Radio Liberty (RFE/RL), current U.S. democracy promotion activities in Russia are perceived to be quite minimal.[31] In general, it is theoretically possible to enlarge the U.S. effort to reach the Russian population by further investing in the Broadcasting Board of Governors or other organizations that communicate directly with the Russian public. In the extreme, Western actions could lead to a new government emerging in Russia that would adopt a less aggressive approach to the West. However, even workshop participants who were generally enthusiastic about expanding democracy promotion activities in eastern Europe and Russia from their current low base—especially because of the human rights abuses of the Russian government—admitted that such actions were unlikely to succeed in changing Russia's political direction. The largest and most obvious downside of this approach is that, from a Russian perspective, "democracy promotion" is equivalent to the kind of internal meddling that Russia is accused of having performed during the 2016 U.S. election. Increased democracy promotion could therefore lead to significant Russian escalation and could work at cross-purposes to other efforts to convince Russia that the United States does not pose a threat.

Define and Set Norms for Nation-State Behavior

One workshop participant proposed a corollary approach to deterrence by punishment, by setting clear norms of behavior and undertaking various sanctions when those norms are violated. Such norm-setting seeks

---

[31] RFE/RL is a U.S. government–funded media outlet that reports news in countries where free press is either restricted by the government or not fully established.

to shape Russia's behavior in two steps: (1) the United States, working with its allies and partners, would articulate what types of behavior are acceptable and which are not and (2) when unacceptable activities take place, the United States and its allies would then take actions against Russia (or any norm violator) accordingly.[32] Norms of state behavior would be accompanied by the establishment of norms of behavior for state-controlled organizations, as noted below. To some degree, U.S. policy to date has been based on this norm-setting approach, but the norms for social media influence operations have not necessarily been fully articulated. Nor are the existing punishments cleanly linked with one specific Russian misbehavior; for example, the 2017 CAATSA legislation that outlined new sanctions against Russia highlighted Russia's actions in Ukraine, preelection influence campaign hacking, and the elements of the broader influence campaign.[33]

Instituting a more thoroughly defined norm-setting approach would involve the U.S. government more clearly articulating norms for nation-state behavior with regards to social media. One possible norm that the U.S. government could adopt would be to oppose covert or deceptive behavior, but accept overt activities. The U.S. government would need to publicly state that overt Russian media organizations, such as RT and Sputnik, were welcome to operate so long as they were properly attributed, and would also need to expand actions to sanction or filter out Russian actors (such as by working with technology companies) who pretend to speak as Americans, such as the IRA. Identifying a specific norm, and sanctioning associated actions made illegitimate by this norm, would hopefully lead Russia to positively reciprocate—it might, for example, convince Russia to allow a U.S.-sponsored network greater access to Russian TV distribution. Workshop participants, including those from technology companies, emphasized that their efforts with regard to Russian actors on social media have been focused on reducing deceptive activities, based partly on the idea that overt Russian campaigns are less likely to be influen-

---

[32] Requiring both detection and attribution, as mentioned previously, can be quite difficult.

[33] Public Law 115-44, Countering America's Adversaries Through Sanctions Act, August 2, 2017.

tial. Any findings that Moscow authorized activities that violate such norms could justify a range of different, ideally prespecified, punishments, which would complement punishments for Russian proxies, which we discuss later in this report. Aside from the norm to oppose covert or deceptive behavior, there may be alternative norms that the U.S. government could articulate and enforce to limit Russian social media behavior.

A major advantage that this norm-based approach would have over the more general punishment approach is that, in all likelihood, it would receive greater support from U.S. allies, at least if the United States adopted a norm against covert or deceptive behavior. Strengthening this norm could also significantly reduce Russia's belief that punishments undertaken by the United States are arbitrary or capricious, and thereby potentially shift Russia's behavior toward activities that may be perceived as more acceptable. However, the disadvantage to a norm-based approach is that there is no guarantee that Russia would abide by whatever norms the United States and its allies try to establish, and it may be difficult to determine to what extent Russia is in fact abiding by such norms, at least in a timely fashion. Furthermore, the United States would also need to tolerate activities below the established threshold and would be limited from pursuing activities above the stated threshold. Should the United States or its allies fail to abide by the established norms, it would risk justified claims of hypocrisy.

Negotiate an Agreement with Russia

The final approach to shaping Russia's decisionmaking would be coming to a shared agreement with Russia to limit its aggressive activities. One participant recommended that the United States "deal diplomatically with the Russians and try to resolve the issues that push them to pursue these campaigns"—e.g., the Ukraine crisis, the conflict in Syria, and other areas of contention between the United States and Russia. This type of comment reflects a perspective expressed by several participants that Russia's motivation for undertaking aggressive actions on social media reflects its dissatisfaction with a wider range of U.S. policy. One participant suggested that punishment and diplomacy could be combined—economic sanctions could be used as a lever to "nudge Russia to become a bit more economically unstable, which could foster a pressing concern in the Kremlin and bring them to the table." In some respects, an agreement represents a bilateral, formalized version of the previous norm-setting approach, because it would involve a mutually agreed-upon policy to prohibit some activities and legitimize others.

Russia has already proposed two diplomatic efforts that would limit its interference. BuzzFeed reported that, in July 2017, Russia proposed "a sweeping noninterference agreement between Moscow and Washington that would prohibit both governments from meddling in the other's domestic politics." This proposal was built, in part, on the history of the U.S.-Soviet relationship: Specifically, in 1933, the United States agreed to recognize the Soviet Union, in exchange for a pledge by the Soviet Union not to interfere in U.S. politics. However, U.S. officials reportedly responded to the July proposal with "thank you very much, but now is not the time for this"; this response was likely in part because of domestic political challenges in the United States and the high cost to U.S. activities abroad. One U.S. official explained that the agreement would involve "[giving] up democracy promotion in Russia, which we're not willing to do."[34] By April 2018, Russian officials had declined to "give any unilateral statements or assurances" that they would not interfere in the 2018 midterm elections in the United States.[35] Russia has previously explored diplomatic solutions to information activities in the form of the Russian- and Chinese-backed International Code of Conduct for Information Security, which sought to regulate the flow of information across borders in a way that Western countries found to be a "threat to fundamental human rights."[36]

---

[34] John Hudson, "No Deal: How Secret Talks with Russia to Prevent Election Meddling Collapsed," *BuzzFeed News,* December 8, 2017. We note that, from an impartial perspective, democracy promotion in Russia is in many ways equivalent to the meddling that Russia is accused of in the United States.

[35] "Russia Refuses to Guarantee Non-Interference in US Elections," *UAWire,* April 23, 2018.

[36] NATO Cooperative Cyber Defence Centre of Excellence, "Shanghai Cooperation Organization," undated.

The potential advantage of an agreement limiting future information operations is that it might indeed reduce Russia's activities. Protecting against social media influence could be a foreign policy for which there is no easy defense, so mutual agreement might be a desirable outcome. However, there are at least three potential disadvantages and risks of a diplomatic policy. First, from a domestic political point of view, an agreement with Russia might be impractical, given the widely held view that Russia was the aggressor in the 2016 disinformation campaign. An agreement would also create a degree of moral equivalence with U.S. activities in Russia and Russian activities in the United States, which many Americans would find inappropriate. Second, an agreement with Russia would, most likely, involve cutting back desirable U.S. foreign policy activities, especially democracy promotion. However, the impact of cutting back democracy promotion could be minimal: There are few such activities, some of those activities might not be suspended, and ongoing activities are not perceived to be particularly effective at accomplishing major changes in Russian policy. Third, Russia might not abide by such an agreement, and verification could be difficult. Even though it could be difficult to verify that Russia is not interfering in U.S. elections in real time, there may be telltale signs of Russian influence that can be observed in retrospect and responded to, which may alleviate some of the verification challenges.[37]

Participants highlighted the need to improve U.S. government coordination to make any and all of these policies more effective. Any of these policies, but especially the punishment one, require clear communication across the U.S. government about what particular activities mean and which actors undertake them. To this end, one participant argued for "an NSC [National Security Council]–level directorate that focuses on strategy coordination." Closer coordination with allies was also cited as important, although the precise impact of coordinated allied behavior, rather than just U.S. activities, remains uncertain.

---

[37] For more commentary on such an agreement, see, for example, Jack Goldsmith, "The Downsides of Mueller's Russia Indictment," *Lawfare*, February 19, 2018; and Jack Goldsmith, "On the Russian Proposal for Mutual Noninterference in Domestic Politics," *Lawfare*, December 11, 2017.

Limiting Russian Proxies

There are multiple approaches for countering, limiting, or otherwise hindering the ability of Russian proxies to operate and inject disinformation into the social media stream—the second link in the disinformation chain. Recall from the discussion in Chapter One that we identified four categories of Russian proxies; we identified promising or plausible measures that fit into those categories:

- better detecting and identifying Russian proxies
- publicizing entities identified as Russian proxies
- deterring or curtailing activities of known Russian proxies
- reducing proxies' credibility by defining and monitoring norms of behavior relevant to media outlets, social media content, and social media platforms.

Better Detecting and Identifying Russian Proxies

The first step to countering Russian proxies is finding out who they are. While some are currently known, the universe of actors and entities functioning as proxies for Russian influence operations is, by all indications, quite sizable, and identifying them requires considerable investigative efforts.[38] Such identification includes research (particularly using big data tools), focused investigative efforts, and intelligence collection and analysis. Big data research into the operations of Russian information manipulation has been expanding.[39] These efforts typi-

---

[38] Among other examples, PropOrNot claimed it found "over 200 distinct websites, YouTube channels, and Facebook groups which qualify as Russian propaganda outlets" that have "regular U.S. audiences," including "at least 15 million Americans" (Is It Propaganda or Not, 2016). According to an assessment by a European official, the Kremlin "appears to finance a number of less-visible news outlets around the world," citing one survey that had mapped thousands of Russia-linked channels in dozens of countries. This information is based on Garrett M. Graff, "A Guide to Russia's High Tech Tool Box for Subverting US Democracy," *Wired*, August 13, 2017.

[39] See, for example, Todd C. Helmus, Elizabeth Bodine-Baron, Andrew Radin, Madeline Magnuson, Joshua Mendelsohn, William Marcellino, Andriy Bega, and Zev Winkelman, *Russian Social Media Influence: Understanding Russian Propaganda in Eastern Europe*, Santa Monica, Calif.: RAND Corporation, RR-2237-OSD, 2018; Javier Lesaca, "Why Did Russian Social Media Swarm the Digital Conversation About Catalan Independence?" *Wash-*

cally reveal individual social media accounts (bots, trolls, or unwitting disseminators) and their networks, which are used to amplify the message originated by the proxies. But the same research can also help identify proxies and their agents; these include organizations or websites whose links to the Russian state are hidden, other "troll factories," and individual content producers and distributors.

Identifying Russian state proxies will have to be a foundational, ongoing component of both government and nongovernment response to Russian influence-peddling on social media. Many voices, both at the RAND workshop and in our literature review, noted that information-sharing between the U.S. government and technology companies is crucial to successfully identifying malign actors. Social media companies will be better positioned to identify their platforms' vulnerabilities if they are better informed about how the platforms have been abused. Governmental and private sector support for independent research efforts in this space are likewise important.[40] We further highlight the need for coordination in the following section on amplification channels.

But there are several challenges that complicate the identification of Russian proxies, including the attribution problem, adversary adaptations, and restrictions on intelligence-sharing. Tracing opaque organizations to the Russian state, and tying individual social media accounts to an organized effort acting on behalf of the Russian state, remains a challenge. The adversary is a moving target, because Russian actors will adapt to countermeasures, create or co-opt new willing proxies, or migrate to more-permissive platforms. Given these challenges, intelligence-gathering would thus need to be forward-looking and focused on identifying these adaptions or new entities as they emerge. Nongovernmental research efforts are limited in their ability to detect new actors without a firm footprint in digital data or traceable information about those actors' provenance. Classification and restric-

---

ington Post, November 22, 2017; Alliance for Securing Democracy, "Securing Democracy Dispatch," February 26, 2018.

[40] For another proposal regarding support "for bipartisan nongovernmental-organization efforts," see Blackwill and Gordon, 2018.

tions on sharing information also limit the extent to which the government can cooperate with technology companies to identify threats. Indeed, at present, reliable information about Russian operations more often than not becomes public only after the fact.

Despite these challenges, the age-old prescription of knowing one's enemies still applies. And none of these challenges represents an argument against measures to identify Russian proxies. But these challenges do suggest that U.S. efforts are unlikely to be completely successful and fully keep pace with Russian proxies.

Publicizing Entities Identified as Russian Proxies

After identifying Russian proxies, the U.S. government or other actors could adopt an approach of disseminating or publicizing those identified as proxies for the Russian state. Workshop participants describe this approach as "naming and shaming," which resonates with the often-made prescription to name and denounce Russian actors.[41] But discussion and analysis with our participants suggested that the important aspect of this approach is the transparency that comes from naming these proxies, rather than shaming them into changing their behavior, an endeavor that is unlikely to succeed.[42] Publicly revealing proxies provides the information that the American audience needs to appraise information given its source, without shutting down the proxies.[43] Identifying Russian actors also allows legitimate media outfits to avoid picking up Russian propaganda, and social media companies to monitor and take corrective action if warranted.[44] This kind

---

[41] See, for example, Keir Giles, *Countering Russian Information Operations in the Age of Social Media*, New York: Council on Foreign Relations, November 21, 2017.

[42] As Jack Goldsmith recalls President Barack Obama's 2016 observation, "[t]he idea that somehow public shaming is going to be effective . . . doesn't read the thought process in Russia very well" (Goldsmith, 2018).

[43] See, for example, Giles, 2017.

[44] For example, as NBC News reports, "Wake Up America" was revealed as the newest, lower-quality outfit backed by Russia, which immediately ran into difficulties with finding an audience: Facebook removed its page, and Twitter has reportedly imposed restrictions on its account. Ben Collins and Brandy Zadrozny, "This Man Is Running Russia's Newest Propaganda Effort in the U.S.—or at Least He's Trying To," *NBC News*, June 15, 2018.

of transparency was the hallmark of the historical U.S. approach: As a recent review of U.S. efforts to counter Soviet propaganda notes, the United States has met with success "when it took the time to publicize what Soviet propagandists were doing and why," such that people were informed about "attempts to deceive them."[45]

Publicizing Russian proxies can be accomplished through a variety of complementary policies. The Foreign Agent Registration Act (FARA) is one obvious vehicle for labeling proxies as such.[46] FARA requires entities that meet the definition of foreign agent to register, report their foreign funding and their U.S. contacts, and label materials they distribute with "a conspicuous statement that the information is disseminated by the agents on behalf of the foreign principal."[47] Indeed, the purpose of FARA is "to insure that the U.S. Government and the people of the United States are informed of the source of information (propaganda) and the identity of persons attempting to influence U.S. public opinion, policy, and laws."[48]

Workshop participants saw the potential utility of a FARA label, but many noted that the current FARA regime has shortcomings. One shortcoming is that FARA appears to be underenforced and is perceived to be selectively applied.[49] FARA enforcement actions have been rare in the contemporary era, and if violations—such as failure to appropriately label materials—are not being investigated or sanctioned, then the law loses much of its effect.[50] Moreover, workshop

---

[45] Ashley Deeks, Sabrina McCubbin, and Cody M. Poplin, "Addressing Russian Influence: What Can We Learn from U.S. Cold War Counter-Propaganda Efforts?" *Lawfare*, October 25, 2017, citing Dennis Kux, "Soviet Active Measures and Disinformation: Overview and Assessment," *Parameters*, Vol. XV, No. 4, January 1985.

[46] Public Law 75-583, Foreign Agents Registration Act, 1938.

[47] DoJ, "General FARA Frequency Asked Questions," August 21, 2017.

[48] DoJ, 2017.

[49] Steve Vladeck, "A Primer on the Foreign Agents Registration Act—and Related Laws Trump Officials May Have Broken," *Just Security*, April 3, 2017.

[50] For more on enforcement trends, see Michael Shapiro and Diana Tsutieva, moderators, "The Rise of Foreign Agent Laws: The Emerging Trends in Their Enactment and Application in the U.S., Russia and Across the Globe," panel at the annual meeting of the American Bar Association, Washington, D.C., April 20, 2018.

participants argued that FARA has been selectively applied: If RT and Sputnik remain the only foreign "news" media on the roster, the label may lose some of its force. Thus, to the extent workshop participants supported FARA, they also supported improvements to it, such as the ones contained in the currently proposed bills in Congress, which strengthen DoJ's investigative and enforcement arsenal.[51]

There are also proposals to introduce legislation or enact policies to identify the sources of particular kinds of content. Examples of such include the proposed Honest Ads Act, which would require social media companies to disclose the identities of those paying for political ads on their platforms, and unilateral policies by social media companies to identify content as originating from or paid for by Russian proxies.[52] Criminal prosecutions, where possible, can also serve a transparency function: For example, the IRA indictment publicly explained to the American people, with a new level of detail, how exactly this Russian proxy was able to take advantage of American vulnerabilities.[53] Efforts by social media companies to inform users targeted by known Russian proxies have similar effects.

But public naming and other transparency approaches do have considerable drawbacks. While there are fewer implementation challenges than there are for identifying Russian proxies, workshop participants and participants in the broader debate have pointed to Russia's retaliation and uncertain effectiveness as significant drawbacks. For example, Russia responded to the mandate to register RT and Sputnik under FARA by forcing Voice of America, RFE/RL, and seven other outlets backed by the U.S. government to register as foreign agents, which apparently had a powerful chilling effect on Russian outlets,

---

[51] For more information on such proposals, see American Bar Association, 2018, discussing Senate Bill 1679 (2017), the Foreign Agent Lobbying Transparency Enforcement Act, which seeks "to impose graduated civil fines for multiple offenses under FARA," and Senate Bill 625 (2017), the Foreign Agents Registration Modernization and Enforcement Act, which seeks "to provide the Attorney General with the investigative tools to identify and prosecute foreign agents who seek to circumvent Federal registration requirements and unlawfully influence the political process."

[52] Senate Bill 115-1989, "Honest Ads Act," introduced October 19, 2017.

[53] See Collins and Zadrozny, 2018.

which ceased rebroadcasting Voice of America and RFE/RL material.[54] Thus, the cost of continuing to call out Russian actors as foreign agents may well be the demise of the dissemination of independent media voices within Russia.[55]

Moreover, the effects of transparency are not unambiguous. For U.S. audiences with whom Russian content resonates, revelation of its source may well have no effects on its consumption, spread, and stated beliefs.[56] Indeed, even knowing that RT and Sputnik are serving the Kremlin's purposes does not deter Americans from participating in or watching its shows.[57] Calling out Russian propaganda may generate even more attention to it, thus paradoxically amplifying the proxies' message. Some have argued against public attribution, on the grounds that it "may enhance the impact of the Russian information operation" by giving Russia credit for successfully waging information warfare.[58] Further still, naming names without a further response that imposes serious consequences reveals weakness.[59] Informing the population about the details of proxies' activities identified through intelligence "runs the risk of exposing one's own information gathering tactics and

---

[54] Emily Bell, "Russian Voices in Western Media Leave Regulators with New Type of Headache," *Guardian,* March 18, 2018.

[55] As one workshop participant pointed out, Russia may well proceed to "attack the few remaining independent media groups within Russia, such as Novaya Gazeta or Dozhd."

[56] The tendency to seek out and believe information that reinforces existing beliefs is well established in psychological literature. As one workshop participant noted, "People often choose to ignore publicly available information, like nutrition labels or information regarding the safety of vaccines, which directly affects their health or safety. There's no reason to believe that this won't be the case for information labeled as Russian in origin."

[57] See, for example, Johnny Kauffman, "Conservative and Liberal Activists Continue to Take to Russian-Backed Media," National Public Radio, June 20, 2018.

[58] Goldsmith, 2018.

[59] See Goldsmith, 2018; similar considerations lead to the argument that cyberattacks should not be attributed under some conditions. See Benjamin Edwards, Alexander Furnas, Stephanie Forrest, and Robert Axelrod, "Strategic Aspects of Cyberattack, Attribution, and Blame," *PNAS,* Vol. 114, No. 11, February 2017, pp. 2825–2830.

techniques to the adversary."[60] Finally, we note that the American population is far from homogeneous. To be effective, attempts to discredit particular sources must be done in a subtle and nuanced way and tailored to the interests or concerns of each community affected. Most importantly, exposure of a disinformation source within a particular community needs to include a discussion of the immediate harm that trusting that source would cause for that particular community.

Taken together, these considerations counsel caution in deploying policies to achieve transparency. It appears prudent to weigh the benefits of informing the public in particular cases or in particular ways against the likely impact of retaliation, inadvertent amplification of the proxies' message, the appearance of weakness, and the benefits to Russia from attribution and greater understanding of U.S. intelligence-gathering processes. It is unlikely that complete transparency—or transparency by any and every means—would emerge as the best response to every influence campaign waged by Russian proxies.

Deterring or Curtailing Activities of Known Proxies

The next approach seeks to deter identified Russian proxies from future bad behavior or limit their ability to engage in bad behavior. This includes sanctions on the relevant entities and individuals, as well as asset seizures, visa bans, and criminal prosecutions where evidence of crimes exists.[61] In theory, this approach could deter future bad conduct, but it also makes it more difficult for the targeted actors to engage in information operations through social media in the United States. Sanctions, for example, will complicate the targets' purchase of ads on social media, among other things.[62] Criminal prosecutions, while highly unlikely to end in convictions, limit defendants' ability

---

[60] Silbren de Jong, Tim Sweijs, Katarina Kertysova, and Roel Bos, *Inside the Kremlin House of Mirrors: How Liberal Democracies Can Counter Russian Disinformation and Societal Interference,* The Hague, Netherlands: The Hague Center for Strategic Studies, 2017, p. 59.

[61] See Blackwill and Gordon, 2018.

[62] See Fried and Polyakova, 2018, p. 8.

to travel, because they risk arrest and extradition, and their ability to operate undetected is also limited.[63]

Another tactic for thwarting Russian proxy activity is, of course, to simply ban known proxies from certain activities. For example, the proposed DISCLOSE Act of 2017, Senate Bill 1585, would ban campaign contributions and expenditures by corporations that are controlled, influenced, or owned by foreign nationals. Acting on its own initiative, Twitter has decided to ban RT and Sputnik from buying any advertising on its platform. The extreme incarnation of this approach is to ban known proxies from social media platforms altogether. Among workshop participants, outright bans were a less-favored tactic, because bans raise the specter of censorship (especially when done by the government) and were deemed likely to cause a backlash effect.[64] Furthermore, even when not done by a government actor, such approaches are at odds with America's free speech values.[65]

Sanctions and similar targeted measures may also draw Russian retaliation. Criminal prosecutions may "reveal something about U.S. intelligence collection methods that will make it easier for the Russians to hide their tracks in the future."[66] And, as already noted, indictments without a real chance at obtaining jurisdiction over the defendants could, above all, telegraph weakness. At the same time, there is uncertainty about how effective such policies are in preventing future operations by Russia's proxies. Policies such as sanctions, prosecutions, or selective bans are likely to be effective at curtailing activities of the targeted proxies—to some extent. But they are unlikely to be effective as a deterrent that reduces the overall level of proxy activity. For

---

[63] See Matt Apuzzo and Sharon LaFraniere, "13 Russians Indicted as Mueller Reveals Effort to Aid Trump Campaign," *New York Times*, February 16, 2018, p. A1.

[64] As one workshop participant noted, nothing reinforces RT's message that it offers news the U.S. government does not want you to hear as much as a government ban that communicates "we don't want you to hear this news."

[65] Hybrid approaches, such as identifying foreign contributors and suspect content with labels or warnings and requiring a confirmation step before sharing, could achieve the same objectives without explicitly banning information.

[66] See Goldsmith, 2018.

instance, sanctions could make it difficult for the targeted actors to operate, but other, nonsanctioned actors are likely to emerge to take their place. The same may be true of selective bans: Banned advertisements by RT and Sputnik, for instance, could be easily replaced by ads bought by as-yet-undiscovered proxies. That said, the uncertainty about ultimate effectiveness is not a decisive argument against opting for these policies; it does, however, suggest the need to moderate expectations when choosing these policies, and counsels against overreliance on these policies alone.

Reducing Proxies' Credibility by Defining and Monitoring Norms of Behavior

Echoing the establishment of norms for state behavior, a final approach described by workshop participants involved defining norms for acceptable and unacceptable behaviors and establishing mechanisms for monitoring compliance. These norms would pertain to professional news organizations (i.e., norms of professional and responsible journalism) and to behavior on social media platforms by groups and individuals (e.g., norms against impersonation and fraudulent identities). Being able to connect Russian proxies to clear violations of norms helps to devalue or demote their credibility relative to norm-adhering entities. Making clear which norms are being violated by openly operating media outfits—as well as entities such as the IRA operating covertly on social media—is also important to the success of policies such as sanctions. If sanctions seek to change behavior, it is helpful to identify which behaviors are at stake. This clarity is likewise important to transparency policies that entail publicizing the identities of Russian proxies, insofar as the goal of publicity is to communicate why and how these actors violate the norms of acceptable behavior in a democratic society. Simply naming and publicizing proxies—such as through FARA registration—does not adequately communicate which norms foreign agents are violating, because being a foreign agent in and of itself is not a norm violation.[67]

---

[67] The stigma from the mere fact of being on the FARA registry is diluted by the fact that the list features many prominent and respected U.S. law firms, who represent foreign principals.

The chief challenge of defining norms for acceptable and unacceptable behaviors, and establishing mechanisms for monitoring compliance, is identifying—or creating—institutions that are sufficiently trusted to articulate norms and serve as arbiters of compliance. In some European countries, a dedicated government agency serves the norm-monitoring function. For instance, in the United Kingdom, Ofcom—the country's communications regulator—has jurisdiction that authorizes it to decide when a media entity has run afoul of discrete norms pertaining to news media and to pursue enforcement against that entity. Ofcom has, in fact, imposed various legal penalties on Russian news providers for spreading information that is "materially misleading" and "not duly impartial," among other violations.[68]

In the United States, First Amendment laws and the country's legal culture pose obstacles to government regulation of content, when compared with the United Kingdom or countries with a similar regulator. If feasible at all, an institution with the capacity to define norms and monitor violations would require an independent, nongovernmental effort. Social media companies themselves have been rolling out programs to identify some kinds of "fake news," which is a form of norm definition and monitoring.[69] Demands for social media companies to take actions to police their platforms in the United States are legion.[70] But social media efforts alone are insufficient. This is, in part, because of "the extent to which [existing] initiatives capture

---

[68] Jasper Jackson, "RT Sanctioned by Ofcom over Series of Misleading and Biased Articles," *Guardian*, September 21, 2015. Ofcom is even considering revoking RT's broadcast license in the wake of the Skripal poisoning. This information is based on Cat Rutter Pooley, "Ofcom Puts Kremlin-Backed Broadcaster RT's UK Licences Under Review," *Financial Times*, May 13, 2018.

[69] See, for example, Helmus et al., 2018:

> Facebook, for example, has developed a "disputed tag" that warns users that online fact-checkers or Facebook's own algorithms have identified the content as suspect. Google offers a Fact Check tag that it applies to suspect content displayed on the Google News portal. Neither Facebook nor Google labels the stories as true or false. Twitter, alternatively, offers its verified account system. Essentially, an account that has been vetted to ensure that it represents whom it says it does receives a blue check mark next to the account name.

[70] See, for example, Giles, 2017.

Russian-promulgated content remains to be seen," as a recent RAND report points out.[71] It is also because social media companies are profit-seeking entities, and thus it may be difficult for them to establish the requisite level of public trust and credibility. Given this, proposals like Clint Watts's suggestion of setting up an "information consumer reports agency," which would have to "reside outside the social media companies, have no contact with the government and should be a non-profit entity."[72] Such an agency could, for example, rate information outlets on the basis of their *fact to fiction* and *reporting to opinion* ratios. Moreover, one important function of a norm-monitoring agency could be monitoring social media companies' efforts and processes to police their own platforms. In view of the degree of dissatisfaction with social media companies' handling of Russian information operations to date, as evidenced by the numerous congressional hearings held on the matter, an independent and trusted institution that can assess whether social media companies themselves are living up to appropriate norms may be well advised.

Creating a credible norm-monitoring institution is worth considering as a longer-term measure. A key challenge in this task is identifying—or creating—institutions that are sufficiently trusted to be the articulators of norms and arbiters of compliance. Trusted institutions cannot be created overnight. And a truly independent institution would require collaboration between government and nongovernmental entities, and currently, an obvious candidate for an organization to take the lead in the creation of such institutions does not exist. Another challenge is that even a nongovernmental institution would need to navigate the challenge of defining meaningful norms without excessively infringing on the robust norms of free speech in the United States. As one of the workshop participants observed, "a lot of Americans would be horrified with what Ofcom does."

---

[71] See, for example, Helmus et al., 2018.

[72] Watts, 2017.

Reducing the Effect of Amplification Channels

The third set of solutions we consider focuses on reducing the effect of amplification channels, both of platforms and individuals, that serve to spread disinformation. We identified promising or plausible approaches that fit into three categories, which are aimed at the following:

- developing and sharing tools to detect and combat disinformation
- coordinating detection of disinformation
- limiting the spread of disinformation on social media platforms.

Developing and Sharing Tools to Detect and Combat Disinformation

During our workshop, participants identified the need to design and share tools between private companies, government, and academia—specifically, algorithms, data, and software that can identify disinformation, verify credible sources, counter disinformation, and promote credible sources.[73] Machine-learning–based classifiers are already being used to detect potential disinformation on Facebook and other platforms. Research teams at private companies and in academia could work to improve the algorithms that detect bots and fake accounts, or even correlate them across platforms. Tools that enhance verification of accounts and improve attribution of the sources of both accounts and advertisements could give consumers more information. Changes to algorithms for promoting or demoting certain stories would also fall under this heading, but platforms must be transparent about their design and implementation. A successful suite of tools would result in more-empowered consumers and increased transparency of how platforms operate, leading to the ultimate goal of spreading less disinformation.

---

[73] Giles, 2017; Nick Summers, "Google Will Flag Fake News Stories in Search Results," *Engadget*, April 7, 2017; Hal Berghel, "Oh, What a Tangled Web: Russian Hacking, Fake News, and the 2016 US Presidential Election," *Computer*, Vol. 50, No. 9, September 2017, pp. 87–91; and Vidya Narayanan, Vlad Barash, John Kelly, Bence Kollanyi, Lisa-Maria Neudert, and Philip N. Howard, *Data Memo No. 2018.1, Polarization, Partisanship, and Junk News Consumption over Social Media in the U.S.*, Computational Propaganda Project, February 6, 2018.

This approach relies primarily on social media platforms designing, implementing, and making such tools transparent, which may decrease the platforms' competitiveness in a challenging market.[74] It also raises the issue that adversaries will take advantage of the increased transparency and change their behavior to evade detection, thus resulting in a similar arms race that has already occurred in efforts to combat spam. All in all, the approach of developing and sharing tools is promising, but the ability to make them transparent (and thus verifiable) may be challenging.

Coordinating Detection of Disinformation

The issue of detecting actors spreading disinformation and distinguishing disinformation from valid content is similar to the problem of identifying and detecting Russian proxies. Without first knowing who or what is the problem, social media companies and other organizations cannot create solutions to reduce the impact of disinformation. Increasing cooperation and information-sharing between the private sector, academia, and the government is key to solving this problem. In particular, sharing known characteristics of bots and troll accounts seems to be low-hanging fruit that would not impose too large of a burden on the private sector. Such accounts would most likely behave similarly across platforms, whether in terms of disseminating content at particular times or in mirroring account information. Specifically, social media companies could clarify the extent and impact of Russia's manipulation to the best of their ability, rather than the current approach of closing off their platforms and limiting the historical data available to researchers. Collecting and comparing that information would enable the social media industry at large to improve its ability to detect such accounts. Academics also play a role here, in that they could and should publicize research aimed at making such identification more accurate and efficient.

Workshop participants strongly agreed that it is the responsibility of the U.S. government to collect and analyze information to help

---

[74] We note that it is possible that private companies could simply create the impression that they are making such changes rather than genuinely doing so, in order to avoid the threat of regulation.

identify malign actors, because it not only has well-established paths for critical input from the intelligence community (in contrast to the private sector) but also has the responsibility to work for the public interest. To this end, Facebook convened a meeting in June 2018 with officials from the FBI, DHS, and other tech companies, including Google, Twitter, Apple, Snap, and others, to develop closer ties with law enforcement to prevent abuse of their platforms.[75] To the extent possible allowed by classification requirements, the U.S. government should share information on adversary accounts, Russian strategy, tactics, and intent with both private companies, academics, and the American public. Despite difficulties that may exist and the perception that government organizations have abrogated their responsibilities, we emphasize that the U.S. government could and should lead efforts in this area, and should not leave the initiative to social media platforms alone.

To coordinate and track these efforts, it might be necessary to establish an independent monitoring organization. Such a working group could be based on similar organizations that promote increasing cybersecurity, or even prior efforts like the Active Measures Working Group (AMWG), established in the 1980s to monitor and expose Soviet disinformation campaigns. A new AMWG-like working group, including participants from government, academia, and, most importantly, the private sector, would coordinate policy and platform solutions with major technology companies, review and propose legislative solutions, and educate the press and the public.[76] Such a government organization could also perform independent research to monitor social media adherence to best practices when it comes to identifying the spreaders of disinformation, providing information, and calling out abuse. We note that this idea is not novel; Rand Waltzman called for a "center for information environment security" in 2015 to leverage the technologies developed by the Defense Advanced Research Proj-

---

[75] See Dwoskin and Nakashima, 2018.

[76] We note that the Portman-Murphy Bill (the Countering Information Warfare Act) included in the 2017 NDAA essentially called for the reconstitution of the AMWG but did not use that name; Deeks et al., 2017.

ects Agency's Social Media in Strategic Communications program to defend U.S. interests in the information environment from all adversaries, including Russia.[77]

For this approach to work effectively, big players (e.g., the FBI and the intelligence community on the government side, and Twitter and Facebook on the private sector side) would need to join and actively participate. The information-sharing must also go both ways. Classification of intelligence is clearly an issue with this approach, and we anticipate some pushback from private companies against the idea of cooperation with the government, especially in terms of sharing proprietary data, private data, or both. Nevertheless, it should be feasible to structure the information-sharing in such a way that it does not require massive data collection or transfer. Massive data collection is unlikely to be effective, let alone amenable to partners. The focus of the information-sharing would be on the Russian threat; adversary tactics, techniques, and procedures; and potential platform and policy solutions. Building and restoring trust between different players will be key to this effort, and successful implementation of such an information-sharing organization would result in greater cooperation between industry and the U.S. government, thus overcoming the gaps with current efforts.

Limiting Spread of Disinformation on Social Media Platforms

One promising approach is for the platforms themselves to take actions to limit the spread of disinformation. Workshop participants suggested that it was particularly important to change the algorithms that promote certain posts above others, thus making things like Facebook's News Feed or Twitter's Trending Topics less susceptible to gaming by various mechanisms, like artificial retweets. Algorithms that identify and deemphasize content promoted by bots would also be useful. Each platform could tailor the tools developed and shared through the approach in the previous section to their specific needs. Platforms

---

[77] Rand Waltzman, "The Weaponization of the Information Environment," *American Foreign Policy Council Defense Technology Program Brief,* September 2015, pp. 4–6. See also Rand Waltzman, "The Weaponization of Information: The Need for Cognitive Security," Santa Monica, Calif.: RAND Corporation, CT-473, April 27, 2017.

could also focus on promoting reliable and vetted news, based on a professional code of conduct that content providers agree to abide by, or use some other tool that measures the veracity of information.

The major disadvantage of this approach is the potential for reduced freedom of speech on these platforms. Relying on algorithms, people, or some combination of the two will introduce bias into the process of deciding what should be kept versus removed or promoted versus demoted. There is no good way around this challenge, because no process or algorithm is perfect, and because inevitably mistakes will be made. It also raises the issue that platforms could become arbiters of truth—a clearly undesirable outcome. The key will be transparency, a willingness to adapt and refine the process based on feedback from users, and partnership with trusted third-party fact-checkers. Based on the difficulties that ongoing efforts are facing, such as Facebook's "remove, reduce, and inform" method, transparency is likely to be the most challenging aspect of this approach; this is highlighted by the confusion and controversy surrounding the implementation of Facebook's current policy.[78] Nevertheless, successful implementation of this approach will result in healthier and more-constructive discussions on a variety of topics on social media platforms.

Another approach is for platforms to limit the ability of advertisers to microtarget users, specifically the ability of political advertisers to target certain groups, which would reduce the ability for Russian proxies and organs to reach specific audiences. Doing this, however, has an obvious downside, given that social media companies rely on this ability for their advertising revenue, which drives most, if not all, of their profits. A potential compromise based on the European General Data Protection Regulation would be for companies to treat political and philosophical data about users as sensitive information, requir-

---

[78] Farhad Manjoo, "What Stays on Facebook and What Goes? The Social Network Cannot Answer," *New York Times*, July 19, 2018, p. A1; Hamza Shaban, "Why Mark Zuckerberg Says Facebook Won't Ban Infowars and Holocaust Deniers," *Washington Post*, July 18, 2018.

ing express permission from users for data collection and targeting of political advertising.[79]

All these policies raise the issue of enforcement. The government does not own social media companies and cannot force them to implement any of these potential solutions. Thus, under the status quo, such solutions must originate with social media companies on their own terms, and the tension between the companies' interests and the public interest in combating disinformation simply cannot be wished away. It is possible that the threat of government regulation could incentivize companies to act expeditiously to preempt that possibility. At the same time, there are discrete opportunities for Congress to legislate with regard to some dimension of the problem, with the Honest Ads Act being a prime example.

Improving Consumer Knowledge and Judgment

There are multiple avenues for improving the ability of consumers to identify and reject Russian disinformation. We identified three promising approaches:

- improving consumer judgment through media literacy campaigns
- working with influencers to help inform key audiences
- studying the impact of social media disinformation.

Improving Consumer Judgment Through Media Literacy Campaigns

Breakout groups in this workshop session spent the largest share of their time discussing media literacy. During the 2016 election, the public witnessed what seemed to be a meteoric rise in the prevalence of fake news. A number of fake stories went viral on Facebook, Twitter, and other social media platforms, including, for example, the blatantly false story that a secret society of pedophiles operated out of a Washington, D.C.–based pizzeria.[80] Social sciences research confirms

---

[79] Karen Kornbluh, "The Internet's Lost Promise," *Foreign Affairs*, September/October 2018.

[80] BBC Trending, "The Saga of 'Pizzagate': The Fake Story That Shows How Conspiracy Theories Spread," *BBC News*, December 2, 2016.

the significance of this problem; several recently conducted studies of American youth showed that many individuals struggle to discriminate between fake and accurate online content.[81] It is within this environment that Russia launched its influence campaign.

Thus, it is not surprising that the idea of media literacy training has taken hold. Such training seeks to improve an audience's ability to access, analyze, evaluate, and even create various forms of media.[82] At a minimum, such training would help recipients better evaluate sources and their potential biases, separate opinion from fact, evaluate and potentially validate the truthfulness of content. If trainees can do this effectively, it could significantly limit the ability of an adversary to effectively use fake news and other disinformation tactics.

Media literacy training is growing on an international scale, with countries like Canada, Australia, and Sweden incorporating media literacy training into their youth education systems.[83] The nonprofit organization IREX, as part of its Learn to Discern program, administered half-day trainings to over 450 adults in Ukraine to help citizens "recognize and resist disinformation, propaganda and hate speech."[84] Several other civil society organizations are pursuing similar approaches, such as the News Literacy Project.[85] Facebook has also launched an advertising campaign to raise awareness of media literacy. One ad in the British press, for example, offered an article titled "Tips for Spotting False News" and identified ten features of fake news to look out for.[86]

Media literacy training programs are also growing, albeit slowly, in the United States. First, a growing number of states have either

---

[81] Joseph Kahne and Benjamin Bowyer, "Educating for Democracy in a Partisan Age: Confronting the Challenges of Motivated Reasoning and Misinformation," *American Educational Research Journal,* Vol. 51, No. 1, 2017, pp. 3–34.

[82] Center for Media Justice, "Resource Library," website, undated.

[83] Dana Priest and Michael Birnhaum, "Europe Has Been Working to Expose Russian Meddling for Years," *Washington Post,* June 25, 2017.

[84] Lisa Guernsey, "A New Program Has Helped Bring Better Media Literacy to Ukraine," *Slate,* May 9, 2018.

[85] The News Literacy Project, website, 2018.

[86] "Facebook Publishes Fake News Ads in UK Papers," *BBC News,* May 8, 2017.

passed or are considering passing laws to support media literacy in the education system. In 2015, Connecticut passed a law requiring education in public schools on safe social media use starting the following year, and the state recently required the formation of the Digital Citizenship, Internet Safety and Media Literacy Advisory Council that will advise the U.S. Department of Education on media literacy training best practices.[87] Other bills to promote media literacy have been passed in Washington, California, New Mexico, and Rhode Island, and legislation is in progress and pending in many other states.[88]

Other initiatives are more focused. Facebook, for example, has launched a campaign that uses both Facebook posts and newspaper ads to provide consumers tips on how to identify fake news.[89] It is intended to reach 170 million people.[90] In addition, IREX is currently working to extend its Learn to Discern program from Ukraine to the United States. And there are many other such programs that range from single-session academic supplement programs to specialized online and offline courses for academics, journalists, and the general public.[91]

There are several obvious drawbacks and challenges to a strategy of social media literacy training. First, the efficacy of the training remains unclear. Some initial research suggests that training can be effective. One study showed that youth who had been exposed to media literacy training could better assess message accuracy compared with

---

[87] Connecticut State Senate, An Act Creating an Advisory Council Relating to Digital Citizenship, Internet Safety and Media Literacy, Public Act No. 17-67, June 27, 2017.

[88] Media Literacy Now, "Connecticut Has New Media Literacy and Digital Citizenship Law," June 17, 2017; Media Literacy Now, "Media Literacy Legislative Roundup: 21 Bills, 11 States, 5 New Laws," January 2, 2018; Media Literacy Now, website, undated.

[89] See Facebook Help Center, "Tips to Spot False News," 2018.

[90] Abrar Al-Heeti, "Facebook Will Fight Fake News with Real Newspaper Ads (and More)," *CNET,* May 23, 2018.

[91] The Newseum, for example, provides a searchable tool that can identify numerous such training opportunities (NewseumED, "Browse 1,000s of Lesson Plans, Classes, Digital Artifacts, Historical Events, and other NewseumED tools," undated). In addition, the Center for Media Literacy, the Poynter Institute, and the University of Rhode Island Media Lab—to name a few—all provide an assortment of training and educational resources for media literacy training.

those without such training.[92] IREX, in a 16-month follow-up survey of participants from its Ukrainian media literacy training, showed that these students experienced a slight improvement in their disinformation analytic skills compared with a similarly aged control group.[93] Such results are promising, but limited. We note that most large-scale efforts to educate populations (such as improving literacy rates or mathematical ability) are fraught with difficulty and have questionable efficacy; media literacy is a much more demanding task. Furthermore, as one reviewer noted, media literacy efforts do not account for the fact that most people do not have the time, energy, or desire to put forth the kind of effort that media literacy demands. Most people are susceptible to emotional manipulation that plays on their existing prejudices and biases. While media literacy campaigns will certainly work for some people, it is possible that they will not work for those masses of people who are actually most vulnerable to emotional manipulation, raising doubt that media literacy training will work on large enough numbers of people to seriously address the disinformation dissemination problem. We note that this disadvantage, while significant, does not argue against doing media literacy training—rather, we argue that expectations should be more realistic.

However, more research is clearly needed to assess the short- and long-term impacts of different types of training regimens. It will also be important to understand the relative benefits of different types of training.

Second, media literacy training, at least the substantive type of training that can be introduced into education systems, will no doubt take time to produce its intended effect. As one academic participant of our workshop noted, "Media literacy is a very long-term objective."

Third, the size of the United States can pose a significant financial and logistical burden to implementing a media literacy campaign. While social media companies may be able to leverage their platforms to educate their customers, any other public education or media cam-

---

[92] Kahne and Bowyer, 2017.

[93] See Al-Heeti, 2018.

paign to inculcate media literacy skills in a broad populace will cost significant amounts of money.

Despite the potential drawbacks and costs, introducing some form of media literacy training into middle and high schools has obvious value. Teaching students to access information from different sources, evaluate a source's bias, and consider whether it is necessary to confirm the truthfulness of the source all seem to be inherently good lessons and, if nothing else, provide an opportunity for critical thinking exercises. And if the training works as intended, then it should theoretically provide a critical bulwark against fake news in general and Russian disinformation in particular. However, this approach is clearly a long-term solution, and one that is not likely to bear fruit for a number of years.

This leaves open the question of whether any short-term solutions exist that can raise awareness and education in the broad population. Any effort to provide substantive instruction, such as the half-day training provided by IREX's Learn to Discern program, will face an immediate hurdle of scale. It would train too few people to make a substantive difference in the short term. Other efforts, such as Facebook's media literacy advertising campaign, can operate at scale, but can a campaign premised on newspaper or Facebook ads be effective? Ultimately, this is an empirical question, and as with educational media literacy programing, it will be critical to systematically study the short- and long-term effectiveness of different types of training to help government and private sector policymakers make the best choices.

Working with Influencers to Help Inform Key Audiences

A second major approach discussed by the breakout groups focused on working with key influencers. As one participant noted, "We need to amplify third-party voices because the government isn't always considered to be a trusted source. . . . We don't want to categorize any initiatives as 'institutionalization,' because that automatically reduces public trust." Another participant likewise noted, "We need to fund and empower partners and key influencers"—ensuring that disinformation does not go through trusted members of a community.

In RAND's recent publication, *Russian Social Media Influence*, the authors also proposed working with influencers.[94] This recommended solution was focused on Eastern Europe, including the Baltic countries (Estonia, Latvia, and Lithuania) and Ukraine. A fundamental challenge in this region is the strong influence of Russian media. Russian television, news, and websites serve as predominant information sources for many native Russian speakers in the region. One remedy proposed for this issue was to find ways to increase local access to Russian-language, Western-oriented content. We recommended training for local journalists, increasing access to Russian-language television, and working with key influencers. For key influencers, our focus was social media. Specifically, we recommended identifying key and influential Russian-speaking, Western-friendly social media stars. Once identified, local organizations could provide training to improve the influencers' social media and other communication skills, which might, in turn, increase the size of their audience.[95]

This particular angle for working with influencers does not appear applicable to the U.S. landscape. Although there is no lack of content, it could be inappropriate for the U.S. government to identify and train influences—co-ideologues—on social media. So, how might it be possible to strengthen influencers to counter Russian disinformation at home, and which actors should be involved?

First, it may be valuable for local government or NGOs to work with key influencers in local communities to help disseminate critical news and information. For example, if a Russian disinformation story were to gain heavy traction in rural west Texas or a New York City borough, then in addition to relying on traditional top-down communication channels to correct the story, it makes sense for local government or civil society members who have both credibility and a built-in audience to correct the story. This approach is similar to the "countermessaging" or "alternative narrative" strategy often used to counter violent extremist narratives, with the key addition that the refutation of false information is coming from trusted sources within the community.

---

[94] Helmus et al., 2018.

[95] Helmus et al., 2018.

Second, it could be possible for government organizations or NGOs to provide certain key influencers with media literacy and other training so that they could both identify fake news content within their own social media networks and actively intervene to educate the network and effectively police the disinformation story. For this approach to be effective, either a government or NGO would identify key leaders among online communities, such as from a university's Young Democrats of America club or a neighborhood listserv. In this way, limited funds for media literacy training would be expended on the most influential audiences.

Finally, as noted earlier, it also could be possible for researchers to identify the influential actors through whom disinformation is wittingly—or unwittingly—flowing. Assuming no laws are broken, the key issue is what can be done with such individuals once they are identified. If such individuals violate a social media platform's terms of service, then the platforms may be able to terminate their accounts. For actions that do not meet this threshold, there also could be value in outreach that helps these individuals recognize the negative impact of their actions and reduce the likelihood that they will unwittingly spread disinformation.

The advantage of this solution lies in the ability of modern social media analytics to identify key influencers. Data from Twitter, for example, can be analyzed to identify communities of closely connected Twitter users and rank-order key influencers for those communities.[96] In addition, the commercial marketing industry provides lessons for influencer outreach and recruitment, skills training, and relationship management. RAND, for example, recently published a report that distills lessons from influencer marketing for identifying and working with influencers to counter the Islamic State of Iraq and the Sham, commonly known as ISIS.[97]

---

[96] Helmus et al., 2018.

[97] Elizabeth Bodine-Baron, Todd C. Helmus, Madeline Magnuson, and Zev Winkelman, *Examining ISIS Support and Opposition: Networks on Twitter*, Santa Monica, Calif.: RAND Corporation, RR-1328-RC, 2016.

The biggest drawback and challenge to the strategy of working with influencers is that influencers, by their very nature, are independent. In fact, most influencers gain their credibility through their independence. There is no guarantee that the influencer will follow a party line, respond to government interlocutors as requested, or use any trained skills as intended.

While influencer engagement campaigns can be complicated to execute, there are established policies and practices that can help improve their effectiveness. We thus recommend that the U.S. government, as well as engaged civil society organizations and the technology sector, consider several of the options we have described.

Studying the Impact of Social Media Disinformation

A third major recommended approach is to better understand the drivers and impact of social media disinformation. This approach recognizes that there is a dearth of scientific information that can answer a number of basic questions about vulnerability to disinformation attacks, mechanisms to guard against such attacks, and ways to mitigate the impact of attacks. Specific questions posed by the workshop participants include the following:

- Who is the most susceptible to Russian influence and content?
- What was the impact of Russia's influence campaign?
- How susceptible is the United States to future Russian disinformation attacks?
- Who are the specific targets (demographics) of Russia's influence campaigns?

Facebook also recognizes the need for research; it plans to fund researchers to investigate the volume and effects of disinformation on its platform.[98] RAND's Jennifer Kavanagh and Michael D. Rich, in their recently published *Truth Decay*, dedicated an entire chapter on

---

[98] See Al-Heeti, 2018.

identifying a research agenda that can help guide the debate about Truth Decay and help shape policy responses.[99]

The strengths and weaknesses of such an approach are fairly self-evident. Developing answers to these and many other questions will prove critical if policymakers, civil society, and the technology sector are to craft effective policy solutions. Such an endeavor will require at least some public funding and certainly time for the research to be initiated, completed, and made publicly available.

Better understanding the impact and process of disinformation is a necessary prerequisite to formulating and, ultimately, improving policies that can prevent its amplification and protect American citizens from its ill effects. To specifically combat the Russian approach to disinformation, the tactics discussed in RAND's *Firehose of Falsehood* report are a useful starting point.[100] Therefore, despite the long-term nature of any research program, it will be critical for the United States, various nonprofit foundations, and the technology sector to fund basic and applied research. To do this effectively, the various potential funding organizations will need to work together to first identify a key research agenda and then coordinate to ensure that the agenda is funded as efficiently as possible and without unnecessary duplication. Recognizing this requirement, the breakout groups agreed that the National Science Foundation will need to play a key and synchronizing role.

---

[99] Jennifer Kavanagh and Michael D. Rich, *Truth Decay: An Initial Exploration of the Diminishing Role of Facts and Analysis in American Public Life*, Santa Monica, Calif.: RAND Corporation, RR-2314-RC, 2018.

[100] Paul and Matthews, 2016.

CHAPTER FOUR

Conclusions and Recommendations

Because no single approach to countering Russian social media influence is likely to produce a conclusive victory over the threat, it is prudent to adopt approaches and associated policies that target multiple links in the chain. Taking a step back and reviewing the various approaches we described, we see several themes emerge that cut across multiple links.

Establish clear and enforceable norms for acceptable behavior for states' and media entities' behavior on social media platforms. Establishing clearer norms for behavior appears to be an important foundational strategy for both shaping Russian decisionmaking and limiting Russia's proxies. Attribution and clarity as to the norms violated and by whom, determined by a credible entity, is vital— regardless of any other approaches chosen to confront these links in the chain, such as punishment or "naming and shaming." If punishments are to be imposed on the Russian government, it is essential that punishments are proportionate to the norm-violating behavior, are sufficiently costly to change the government's approach, and can be discontinued or limited when this behavior ceases. Without proportionality, the chosen punishments risk being too weak to be compelling—or, on the contrary, excessive and therefore producing a backlash effect. Without a clear linkage between the norm-violating behavior and the punishment, the Russian state or its proxies may well see no benefit from changing behaviors. If the goal is simply to name and shame, or expose wrongdoing by Russian proxies, clarity as to the nature of the shameful behavior (that is, the norm) is likewise crucial. The establishment of norms may also be beneficial for broader U.S. foreign policy goals in

Russia and former Soviet countries. In particular, a clear articulation of norms should allow the United States to distinguish its own public and attributed outreach to foreign audiences from the deceptive practices in which Russia and its proxies have engaged, thereby reducing the risk of being seen as hypocritical, and building more-fertile ground for its own public campaigns abroad.

Coordinate U.S. executive and legislative branch activities. Our assessment of current U.S. government approaches identified significant gaps in interagency coordination in the executive branch, as well as a divergence between the activities of the executive and the legislative branch. While there are relevant task forces within several U.S. government agencies, including DHS and DoJ, it is critical to assign overall leadership of the effort to counter Russian social media disinformation (on its own or in combination with other Russian influence activities) to a single department or agency. Given its domestic mandate, this could be the DHS, but also could be another organization, depending on the evolution of other types of regulatory activities over social media companies.

Institute a formal mechanism for information-sharing that includes key players from the U.S. government and private social media companies. While social media companies have control over their platforms, with an ability to filter out or identify suspect accounts and content, the U.S. government often has superior information about Russian strategies, tactics, and adaptations. A formal mechanism for information-sharing would enable social media companies to implement measures earlier, rather than after the execution of a particular influence operation, facilitating both the detection and curtailing of Russian proxies and the reduction of potential amplification channels. Such an institution could be modeled on the AMWG, which enjoyed a measure of success by communicating the characteristics of Soviet disinformation to news media, enabling those outlets to better identify and stop the spread of such material. In the modern version, information would flow both ways: Anonymized social media data would enable government organizations to connect trends to specific disinformation tactics, techniques, procedures, and adversary groups, while tips from those same organizations could help social media companies detect and remove disinformation early. The specific mechanism could take different forms, but at minimum should consist of a standing committee with participants from social media companies, government organizations, the intelligence community, NGOs, and academia. Several ad hoc efforts along these lines have already begun, indicating the willingness of the necessary organizations to share at least some information and the feasibility of creating something more formal.

Increase the transparency of social media platform policies and algorithms for detecting and removing disinformation and malicious behavior. Encourage and fund academia to develop better tools for identifying and attributing disinformation on social media. Social media companies are currently facing pushback from both consumers and government organizations for the role their platforms have played in the spread of disinformation. Increasing the transparency of their algorithms and policies for what content constitutes disinformation, what behaviors violate terms of service agreements, and how content and accounts are demoted or removed will increase consumer confidence in these platforms and potentially preempt the passage of more heavy-handed legislative or regulatory efforts to combat the Russian disinformation threat. A key aspect of transparency is enabling outside observers to verify and validate the approaches technology companies are taking to reduce disinformation—without this increased insight, it would be impossible to know whether private companies are making any difference. Increased transparency of algorithms and data will also enable academic researchers to develop better tools for the identification—and, most importantly, attribution—of disinformation and malicious actors on social media. Together with increased funding from foundations and government organizations like the National Science Foundation, this approach can improve the ability of individuals and platforms to identify disinformation, reducing the appeal of such campaigns for Moscow's decisionmakers, enabling naming and shaming approaches, reducing amplification effects, and better educating consumers.

Prioritize defensive activities over punishments to shape Moscow's decisionmaking. We note that the recommendations highlighted here all focus on defensive, rather than offensive, approaches. While the U.S. government could adopt more-offensive approaches—including through well-developed punishment, elements of democracy promotion, and the development of a negotiated agreement—these approaches all have significant disadvantages and are unlikely to convince Russia to cease its influence campaigns. Improving defense, therefore, has the best hope of reducing the impact of Russian disinformation campaigns on social media. The defensive approaches suggested here (limiting Russian proxies, reducing amplification channels, and educating consumers) are most likely to affect Russian decisionmakers by reducing the perceived effectiveness of disinformation campaigns on social media.

Continuously assess the cost and impact of proposed solutions relative to the effectiveness of Russia's activities. As our discussion suggests, no approach or policy option is without its potential drawbacks or costs. Notably, because Russia's instrument of influence in question entails speech, many efforts to counter Russian activities could be perceived to—or could, in fact—curtail, limit, or chill speech activities. Even when not done by state actors, such effects are in juxtaposition with American legal, political, and social culture. Thus, while Russia's influence campaigns are unwelcome, not all means of addressing them are advisable. Deciding whether to adopt a suggested initiative depends on determining whether the benefit of the initiative, in terms of reducing the effectiveness of Russia's activities, exceeds the associated costs. The difficulty with conducting such a calculus, of course, is that the effectiveness of Russia's campaigns—and thus, the value of thwarting them—is unknown. Thus, in many cases, weighing the potential benefits against the potential costs must remain a somewhat speculative enterprise. Our findings offer an initial account of the potential cost and risk of some potential initiatives, but further and continuous efforts are needed to evaluate the relevant trade-offs.

References

Al-Heeti, Abrar, "Facebook Will Fight Fake News with Real Newspaper Ads (and More)," *CNET,* May 23, 2018. As of June 1, 2018:
https://www.cnet.com/news/facebook-is-fighting-misinformation-with-news-literacy-campaign-help-from-researchers/

Alliance for Securing Democracy, "Securing Democracy Dispatch," February 26, 2018. As of June 1, 2018:
https://securingdemocracy.gmfus.org/securing-democracy-dispatch-3/

Apuzzo, Matt, and Sharon LaFraniere, "13 Russians Indicted as Mueller Reveals Effort to Aid Trump Campaign," *New York Times*, February 16, 2018, p. A1.

BBC Trending, "The Saga of 'Pizzagate': The Fake Story That Shows How Conspiracy Theories Spread," *BBC News*, December 2, 2016. As of June 1, 2018:
https://www.bbc.com/news/blogs-trending-38156985

Bell, Emily, "Russian Voices in Western Media Leave Regulators with New Type of Headache," *Guardian,* March 18, 2018.

Berghel, Hal, "Oh, What a Tangled Web: Russian Hacking, Fake News, and the 2016 US Presidential Election," *Computer,* Vol. 50, No. 9, September 2017, pp. 87–91.

Blackwill, Robert D., and Philip H. Gordon, *Council Special Report No. 18: Containing Russia: How to Respond to Moscow's Intervention in U.S. Democracy and Growing Geopolitical Challenge*, New York: Council on Foreign Relations, January 2018.

Bodine-Baron, Elizabeth, Todd C. Helmus, Madeline Magnuson, and Zev Winkelman, *Examining ISIS Support and Opposition: Networks on Twitter*, Santa Monica, Calif.: RAND Corporation, RR-1328-RC, 2016. As of June 1, 2018:
https://www.rand.org/pubs/research_reports/RR1328.html

Bowles, Nellie, and Sheera Frenkel, "Facebook and Twitter Plan New Ways to Regulate Political Ads," *New York Times*, May 24, 2018, p. A12.

Center for Media Justice, "Resource Library," undated. As of May 15, 2018:
https://centerformediajustice.org/build-leadership/resource-library/

Chen, Adrian, "The Agency," *New York Times Magazine*, June 2, 2015, p. 57.

Collins, Ben, and Brandy Zadrozny, "This Man Is Running Russia's Newest Propaganda Effort in the U.S.—Or at Least He's Trying To," *NBC News*, June 15, 2018. As of July 10, 2018:
https://www.nbcnews.com/news/us-news/
man-running-russia-s-newest-propaganda-effort-u-s-or-n883736

Connecticut State Senate, An Act Creating an Advisory Council Relating to Digital Citizenship, Internet Safety and Media Literacy, Public Act No. 17-67, June 27, 2017. As of May 15, 2018:
https://www.cga.ct.gov/asp/cgabillstatus/
cgabillstatus.asp?selBillType=Bill&which_year=2017&bill_num=949

Deeks, Ashley, Sabrina McCubbin, and Cody M. Poplin, "Addressing Russian Influence: What Can We Learn from U.S. Cold War Counter-Propaganda Efforts?" *Lawfare*, October 25, 2017. As of June 1, 2018:
https://www.lawfareblog.com/addressing-russian-influence-what-can-we-learn-us-cold-war-counter-propaganda-efforts

de Jong, Silbren, Tim Sweijs, Katarina Kertysova, and Roel Bos, *Inside the Kremlin House of Mirrors: How Liberal Democracies Can Counter Russian Disinformation and Societal Interference,* The Hague, Netherlands: The Hague Center for Strategic Studies, 2017.

Demirjian, Karoun, "Republicans, Democrats Partner on Russia Sanctions Bill, New Cyber Measures," *Washington Post*, August 2, 2018.

DHS—*See* U.S. Department of Homeland Security.

DoJ—*See* U.S. Department of Justice.

Dwoskin, Elizabeth, and Ellen Nakashima, "Tech Didn't Spot Russian Interference During the Last Election: Now It's Asking Law Enforcement for Help," *Washington Post*, June 26, 2018.

Edwards, Benjamin, Alexander Furnas, Stephanie Forrest, and Robert Axelrod, "Strategic Aspects of Cyberattack, Attribution, and Blame," *PNAS*, Vol. 114, No. 11, February 2017, pp. 2825–2830.

Facebook, "Community Standards," webpage, 2018. As of August 1, 2018:
https://www.facebook.com/communitystandards/

Facebook Help Center, "Tips to Spot False News," 2018. As of August 1, 2018:
https://www.facebook.com/help/188118808357379

"Facebook Publishes Fake News Ads in UK Papers," *BBC News*, May 8, 2017.

Farwell, James P., "Countering Russian Meddling in U.S. Political Processes," *Parameters*, Vol. 48, No. 1, Spring 2018, pp. 37–47.

Fly, Jamie, Laura Rosenberger, and David Salvo, *The ASD Policy Blueprint for Countering Authoritarian Interference in Democracies*, Washington, D.C.: German Marshall Fund of the United States, Alliance for Securing Democracy, June 26, 2018.

Fried, Daniel, and Alina Polyakova, *Democratic Defense Against Disinformation*, Washington, D.C.: Atlantic Council, February 2018. As of July 1, 2018:
http://www.atlanticcouncil.org/publications/reports/
democratic-defense-against-disinformation

Galeotti, Mark, *Policy Brief: Controlling Chaos: How Russia Manages Its Political War in Europe*, London: European Council on Foreign Relations, August 2017.

Giles, Keir, *Countering Russian Information Operations in the Age of Social Media*, New York: Council on Foreign Relations, November 21, 2017. As of July 1, 2018:
https://www.cfr.org/report/
countering-russian-information-operations-age-social-media

Goldsmith, Jack, "On the Russian Proposal for Mutual Noninterference in Domestic Politics," *Lawfare*, December 11, 2017. As of May 15, 2018:
https://www.lawfareblog.com/
russian-proposal-mutual-noninterference-domestic-politics

———, "The Downsides of Mueller's Russia Indictment," *Lawfare*, February 19, 2018. As of May 15, 2018:
https://www.lawfareblog.com/downsides-muellers-russia-indictment

Graff, Garrett M., "A Guide to Russia's High Tech Tool Box for Subverting US Democracy," *Wired*, August 13, 2017. As of June 1, 2018:
https://www.wired.com/
story/a-guide-to-russias-high-tech-tool-box-for-subverting-us-democracy/

Guernsey, Lisa, "A New Program Has Helped Bring Better Media Literacy to Ukraine," *Slate*, May 9, 2018. As of June 1, 2018:
https://slate.com/technology/2018/05/can-a-media-literacy-program-that-is-working-in-ukraine-also-help-the-u-s.html

Hanlon, Bradley, "It's Not Just Facebook: Countering Russia's Social Media Offensive," German Marshall Fund of the United States, Alliance for Securing Democracy, April 11, 2018. As of June 1, 2018:
https://securingdemocracy.gmfus.org/
its-not-just-facebook-countering-russias-social-media-offensive/

Helmus, Todd C., Elizabeth Bodine-Baron, Andrew Radin, Madeline Magnuson, Joshua Mendelsohn, William Marcellino, Andriy Bega, and Zev Winkelman, *Russian Social Media Influence: Understanding Russian Propaganda in Eastern Europe*, Santa Monica, Calif.: RAND Corporation, RR-2237-OSD, 2018. As of May 15, 2018:
https://www.rand.org/pubs/research_reports/RR2237.html

Hudson, John, "No Deal: How Secret Talks with Russia to Prevent Election Meddling Collapsed," *BuzzFeed News,* December 8, 2017. As of May 15, 2018: https://www.buzzfeednews.com/article/johnhudson/ no-deal-how-secret-talks-with-russia-to-prevent-election

Indictment, *United States v. Internet Research Agency,* Case 1:18-cr-00032-DLF (D.D.C. Feb. 16, 2018). As of May 15, 2018: https://www.justice.gov/file/1035477/download

Is It Propaganda or Not? *Black Friday Report: On Russian Propaganda Network Mapping,* November 26, 2016. As of September 25, 2018: https://drive.google.com/file/d/0Byj_1ybuSGp_NmYtRF95VTJTeUk/view

Jackson, Jasper, "RT Sanctioned by Ofcom over Series of Misleading and Biased Articles," *Guardian,* September 21, 2015.

Kahne, Joseph, and Benjamin Bowyer, "Educating for Democracy in a Partisan Age: Confronting the Challenges of Motivated Reasoning and Misinformation," *American Educational Research Journal,* Vol. 51, No. 1, 2017, pp. 3–34.

Kauffman, Johnny, "Conservative and Liberal Activists Continue to Take to Russian-Backed Media," National Public Radio, June 20, 2018.

Kavanagh, Jennifer, and Michael D. Rich, *Truth Decay: An Initial Exploration of the Diminishing Role of Facts and Analysis in American Public Life,* Santa Monica, Calif.: RAND Corporation, RR-2314-RC, 2018. As of August 1, 2018: https://www.rand.org/pubs/research_reports/RR2314.html

Kimmage, Michael, "Russian Elegies: Candide Goes to Moscow," *War on the Rocks,* June 13, 2018. As of July 1, 2018: https://warontherocks.com/2018/06/russian-elegies-candide-goes-to-moscow/

Kornbluh, Karen, "The Internet's Lost Promise," *Foreign Affairs,* September/ October 2018.

Dennis Kux, "Soviet Active Measures and Disinformation: Overview and Assessment," *Parameters,* Vol. XV, No. 4, January 1985, pp. 19–28.

Lesaca, Javier, "Why Did Russian Social Media Swarm the Digital Conversation About Catalan Independence?" *Washington Post,* November 22, 2017.

Lyons, Tessa, "Hard Questions: How Is Facebook's Fact-Checking Program Working?" Facebook Newsroom, June 14, 2018. As of August 1, 2018: https://newsroom.fb.com/news/2018/06/hard-questions-fact-checking/

Madrigal, Alexis C., "15 Things We Learned from the Tech Giants at the Senate Hearings," *Atlantic,* November 2, 2017. As of May 15, 2018: https://www.theatlantic.com/technology/archive/2017/11/ a-list-of-what-we-really-learned-during-techs-congressional-hearings/544730/

Manjoo, Farhad, "What Stays on Facebook and What Goes? The Social Network Cannot Answer," *New York Times,* July 19, 2018, p. A1.

Marcellino, William, Meagan L. Smith, Christopher Paul, and Lauren Skrabala, *Monitoring Social Media: Lessons for Future Department of Defense Social Media Analysis in Support of Information Operations*, Santa Monica, Calif.: RAND Corporation, RR-1742-OSD, 2017. As of June 1, 2018:
https://www.rand.org/pubs/research_reports/RR1742.html

Media Literacy Now, website, undated. As of August 29, 2018:
https://medialiteracynow.org/

———, "Connecticut Has New Media Literacy and Digital Citizenship Law," June 17, 2017. As of June 1, 2018:
https://medialiteracynow.org/
connecticut-has-new-media-literacy-and-digital-citizenship-law/

———, "Media Literacy Legislative Roundup: 21 Bills, 11 States, 5 New Laws," January 2, 2018. As of May 15, 2018:
https://medialiteracynow.org/
media-literacy-legislative-roundup-21-bills-11-states-5-new-laws/

Nakashima, Ellen, "Inside a Russian Disinformation Campaign in Ukraine in 2014," *Washington Post,* December 25, 2017.

———, "Justice Department Plans to Alert Public to Foreign Operations Targeting U.S. Democracy," *Washington Post*, July 19, 2018.

Narayanan, Vidya, Vlad Barash, John Kelly, Bence Kollanyi, Lisa-Maria Neudert, and Philip N. Howard, *Polarization, Partisanship, and Junk News Consumption over Social Media in the U.S.*, Oxford, UK: Computational Propaganda Project, Data Memo No. 2018.1, February 6, 2018.

NATO Cooperative Cyber Defence Centre of Excellence, "Shanghai Cooperation Organization," undated. As of June 1, 2018:
https://ccdcoe.org/sco.html

NewseumED, "Browse 1,000s of Lesson Plans, Classes, Digital Artifacts, Historical Events, and other NewseumED tools," undated. As of June 15, 2018:
https://newseumed.org/ed-tools/

News Literacy Project, website, 2018. As of August 1, 2018:
https://newslit.org/

ODNI—*See* Office of the Director of National Intelligence.

Office of the Director of National Intelligence, *Assessing Russian Activities and Intentions in Recent US Elections*, Washington, D.C., ICA 2017-01D, January 6, 2017.

Paul, Christopher, and Miriam Matthews, *The Russian "Firehose of Falsehood" Propaganda Model*, Santa Monica, Calif.: RAND Corporation, PE-198-OSD, 2016. As of May 15, 2018:
https://www.rand.org/pubs/perspectives/PE198.html

Pooley, Cat Rutter, "Ofcom Puts Kremlin-Backed Broadcaster RT's UK Licences Under Review," *Financial Times*, May 13, 2018.

Priest, Dana, and Micahel Birnbaum, "Europe Has Been Working to Expose Russian Meddling for Years," *Washington Post*, June 25, 2017.

Public Law 75-583, Foreign Agents Registration Act, 1938.

Public Law 113-328, The National Defense Authorization Act for Fiscal Year 2017, December 23, 2016.

Public Law 115-44, Countering America's Adversaries Through Sanctions Act, August 2, 2017.

Public Law 115-91, The National Defense Authorization Act for Fiscal Year 2018, December 12, 2017.

Robinson, Linda, Todd C. Helmus, Raphael S. Cohen, Alireza Nader, Andrew Radin, Madeline Magnuson, and Katya Migacheva, *Modern Political Warfare: Current Practices and Possible Responses*, Santa Monica, Calif.: RAND Corporation, RR-1772-A, 2018. As of August 1, 2018: https://www.rand.org/pubs/research_reports/RR1772.html

"Russia Refuses to Guarantee Non-Interference in US Elections," *UAWire*, April 23, 2018. As of June 1, 2018: https://www.uawire.org/ russia-refuses-to-guarantee-non-interference-in-us-elections

Satariano, Adam, "Government 'Cyber Troops' Manipulate Facebook, Twitter, Study Says," *Bloomberg*, July 17, 2017.

———, "Ireland's Abortion Referendum Becomes a Test for Facebook and Google," *New York Times*, May 25, 2018.

Shaban, Hamza, "Facebook Says It Will Start Removing Posts That May Lead to Violence," *Washington Post*, July 19, 2018.

———, "Why Mark Zuckerberg Says Facebook Won't Ban Infowars and Holocaust Deniers," *Washington Post*, July 18, 2018.

Shane, Scott, "The Fake Americans Russia Created to Influence the Election," *New York Times*, September 7, 2017.

Shapiro, Michael, and Diana Tsutieva, moderators, "The Rise of Foreign Agent Laws: The Emerging Trends in Their Enactment and Application in the U.S., Russia and Across the Globe," panel at the annual meeting of the American Bar Association, Washington, D.C., April 20, 2018. As of May 15, 2018: http://apps.americanbar.org/dch/thedl.cfm?filename=/IC855000/newsletterpubs/ The_Rise_of_Foreign_Agent_Laws_The_Emerging_Trends_in_their_ Enactment_and_Application_Program_Outline.pdf

Shields, Todd, "FCC Got 444,938 Net-Neutrality Comments from Russian Email Addresses," *Bloomberg News*, November 29, 2017.

Shubber, Kadhim, "US Extends Sanctions Deadline for EN+, Rusal and Gaz Group," *Financial Times*, May 31, 2018.

Snyder, Glenn Herald, *Deterrence and Defense*, Princeton, N.J.: Princeton University Press, 1961.

Summers, Nick, "Google Will Flag Fake News Stories in Search Results," *Engadget*, April 7, 2017. As of June 1, 2018:
https://www.engadget.com/2017/04/07/google-fake-news-fact-check-search-results/

Turak, Natasha, "Trump to Agree to New Russia Sanctions but Impact Will Be Minimal, Analysts Predict," *CNBC*, January 28, 2018. As of June 1, 2018:
https://www.cnbc.com/2018/01/29/
new-us-russia-sanctions-trump-to-comply-but-impact-will-be-minimal.html

U.S. Department of Homeland Security, Critical Infrastructure Partnership Advisory Council, September 18, 2018. As of September 20, 2018:
https://www.dhs.gov/critical-infrastructure-partnership-advisory-council

U.S. Department of Justice, "General FARA Frequency Asked Questions," August 21, 2017. As of May 15, 2018:
https://www.justice.gov/nsd-fara/general-fara-frequently-asked-questions

———, *Report of the Attorney General's Cyber Digital Task Force*, Washington, D.C., July 2, 2018.

U.S. House of Representatives, *A Borderless Battle: Defending Against Cyber Threats; Hearing Before the Committee on Homeland Security*, Washington, D.C.: U.S. Government Printing Office, 2017.

U.S. Senate Bill S. 115-1989, "Honest Ads Act," introduced 10/19/2017

Vladeck, Steve, "A Primer on the Foreign Agents Registration Act—and Related Laws Trump Officials May Have Broken," *Just Security*, April 3, 2017. As of May 15, 2018:
https://www.justsecurity.org/39493/primer-foreign-agents-registration-act/

Waltzman, Rand, "The Weaponization of the Information Environment," *Defense Technology Program Brief*, Washington, D.C.: American Foreign Policy Council, September 2015, pp. 4–6.

———, "The Weaponization of Information: The Need for Cognitive Security," Santa Monica, Calif.: RAND Corporation, CT-473, April 27, 2017. As of May 15, 2018:
https://www.rand.org/pubs/testimonies/CT473.html

Watts, Clint, "Extremist Content and Russian Disinformation Online: Working with Tech to Find Solutions," Foreign Policy Research Institute, October 31, 2017. As of May 15, 2018:
https://www.fpri.org/article/2017/10/
extremist-content-russian-disinformation-online-working-tech-find-solutions/

Weisburd, Andrew, Clint Watts, and J. M. Berger, "Trolling for Trump: How Russia Is Trying to Destroy Our Democracy," *War on the Rocks*, November 6, 2016. As of May 15, 2018:
https://warontherocks.com/2016/11/
trolling-for-trump-how-russia-is-trying-to-destroy-our-democracy/

Zigmond, Dan, "Machine Learning, Fact-Checkers and the Fight Against False News," Facebook Newsroom, April 8, 2018. As of August 1, 2018:
https://newsroom.fb.com/news/2018/04/inside-feed-misinformation-zigmond/

About the Authors

Elizabeth Bodine-Baron is an engineer specializing in complex networks and systems at the RAND Corporation. She is the associate director of the Force Modernization and Employment Program in RAND Project AIR FORCE and co-directs the RAND Center for Applied Network Analysis and System Science. Her research interests include network analysis and modeling for both domestic and national security issues.

Todd C. Helmus is a senior behavioral scientist at the RAND Corporation. He specializes in strategic communications and social media, and his work focuses on countering Russian disinformation and counter violent extremism.

Andrew Radin is a political scientist at the RAND Corporation. His work at RAND has focused on European security, including studying the prospects for security sector reform in Ukraine; Russian political warfare and measures short of war; the threat of "hybrid" warfare in the Baltics; and the political, economic, and military vulnerabilities of Europe.

Elina Treyger is a political scientist at the RAND Corporation, and is also a lawyer. Her work at RAND spans topics in both domestic policy (justice and homeland security) and national security and international affairs (focused on Russia and Eurasia). Her previous work on Russia investigated the legacy of Soviet population management for post-Soviet societies.